A Special Publication of the Society for Psychological Anthropology

The Ethnography
of
Cannibalism

Edited by PAULA BROWN and DONALD TUZIN

Published by the

Society for Psychological Anthropology
1703 New Hampshire Avenue, N.W.
Washington, D.C. 20009

Production Editor
Meredith Helleberg

ISBN Number: 0-913077-00-3

CONTENTS

Sunt &aliæ bestiolæ inbyxonæ quae
leraces apellatur aurib: asininisaellere
ouino pedib: ouum ÷

Frontispiece. Cannibalistic Giant. Manuscript illumination from the *Marvels of the East*, England, 11th century. Reproduced with permission from the British Library, London.

Editors' Preface

The idea of people eating their own kind has a long, if not precisely honorable, history in the intellectual and folk traditions of the West. As a prospect likely to horrify, fascinate, darkly amuse, or otherwise engage the imagination, cannibalism figures prominently in our myths, legends, and fairy tales. As a foil to our moral sense of ourselves, it has been a vehicle for social and political satire and for soul-searching literary studies into the extremities of human action. Until about one hundred years ago, knowledge of actual cannibal practices rested on a heap of travelers' tales, missionary testimonies, conquerors' apologetics, diplomatic and administrative reports, and the like. In general retrospect, the accuracy and objectivity of many of these accounts is open to doubt; but, from the standpoint of a modern anthropological inquiry into cannibalism, there is another, equally serious disability surrounding the early records, including those which appear most reliable. Those observers, because they preceded the advent of an ethnographic tradition, typically did not give much account of the social and cultural contexts in which institutionalized cannibalism occurred. However factual their reports might be, cannibalism remained for them an object of curiosity.

The irony in this state of affairs is that Herodotus, in what is probably the oldest historical reference to the subject, saw rather plainly that cannibalism should be understood as part of a total way of life. In addition to cannibal acts carried out in isolated fits of rage, revenge, war-lust, and madness, he reports in his *History* (1952) that "man-eating" was habitual among the Massagetae and the Andro-phagi—the latter, presumably, by definition! But the most telling instance of Herodotus' "ethnographic" sensitivity in this regard occurs in a passage (Book III) in which he uses the wisdom of Darius to illustrate the point that custom (or "law") reigns supreme as a gover-

1

nor of human attitudes. Thus, after Darius had ascended to the throne, he

called into his presence certain Greeks who were at hand, and asked — "What he should pay them to eat the bodies of their fathers when they died?" To which they answered, that there was no sum that would tempt them to do such a thing. He then sent for certain Indians, of the race called Callatians, men who eat their fathers, and asked them, while the Greeks stood by, and knew by the help of an interpreter all that was said — "What he should give them to burn the bodies of their fathers at their decease?" The Indians exclaimed aloud, and bade him forbear such language. Such is men's wont herein; and Pindar was right, in my judgment, when he said, "Law is the king o'er all." [1952:97–98]

What Herodotus distantly anticipated was a kind of study that would describe not only how a particular practice, such as cannibalism, is carried out, but also the traditional notions according to which that practice is deemed right and proper by the actors, that is, the sense in which it is culturally meaningful. Not until the late 19th century, however, was a program of sorts proposed. Thus, in the 1892 edition of *Notes and Queries on Anthropology*, we are given a well-considered list of 19 questions to serve as a starting guide to the study of cannibalism (p. 129). Apart from various culinary details, the program urges inquiry into the general circumstances of cannibalism, the ritual or other justifications given for it, the statuses of those involved in the feast, and other matters pertaining to the symbolism of the act.

By this time, however, information was difficult to obtain. Under conditions of empire, the practice was no sooner reported than it was forbidden and the beliefs associated with it suppressed by influential colonial officials and missionaries. This was also, of course, the fate of many other practices — ritual, magic, warfare — which are usually close institutional partners of cannibalism. As opportunities for anthropological study were removed, the popular joke became that the anthropologist would be the cannibal's next victim. Twentieth-century anthropology went on to pursue more accessible interests, and cannibalism was once again relegated to the place of a curiosity.

In recent years, however, cultural anthropologists have at last begun to give the topic serious analytic attention. This development stems partly from the discovery of new facts and partly from the realization that cannibalism — like incest, aggression, the nuclear family, and other phenomena of universal human import — is a promising ground on which to exercise certain theoretical programs. Scholars influenced by psychoanalysis naturally heed the recurrence of cannibal fantasies in dreams, folktales, and clinics, and conclude that the institutionalized eating of human flesh must be the expression of psychically primitive, oral-sadistic impulses (Sagan 1974). Others have favored materialist arguments (Dornstreich and Morren 1974; Harris 1977; Harner 1977), emphasizing the substantial nutritional role of cannibalism in those societies where it is practiced. In a study seemingly designed to inspire controversy, Arens (1979) erroneously asserts that cannibalism as an approved, institutionalized form of behavior has never existed. Without affirming this part of Arens's thesis, one might yet admit the plausibility — at least in certain instances — of the author's suggestion that the common *attribution* of cannibalism is a rhetorical device used ideologically by one group to assert its moral superiority over another.

The present collection of essays grew out of the editors' conviction that a good deal of this global theorizing, although stimulating and doubtless worthwhile in its own right, is decidedly premature; that, despite their lengthy awareness of such customs, and for reasons mentioned above, anthropologists are notably uninformed about cannibalistic ideas and practices in specific cultural settings. The exact character of, say, Aztec cannibalism will probably always remain a matter of conjecture. But there are many other societies closer in time to their cannibal traditions — societies in which living informants still remember how, why, and under what circumstances humans were eaten, or for which the relevant documentation is relatively rich and reliable. As a striking example, the discovery that kuru, a degenerative nervous disease afflicting the Fore of the New Guinea Eastern Highlands, is transmitted through the eating of human tissue (Gajdusek 1977; Lindenbaum 1979), focused widespread scientific attention on cannibal customs and their epidemiological consequences. Other ethnographers working in newly contacted societies of the interior of New Guinea — two of whom are contributors to this volume — have turned up an unprecedented core of materials: the status of the victim as enemy, stranger, friend, or kinsman of the cannibal; the custom's mythic and ritual implications; and its connections with witchcraft and sorcery beliefs and with the powers of flesh-and-blood substances.

These essays are offered in the hope of advancing our knowledge and cultural understanding of this remarkable department of human fact and fantasy. By force of opportunity, geographical representation is heavily weighted in favor of Melanesia. Consistent with the ethnographic spirit of the enterprise, but through no particular design of the editors, each of the studies utilizes one or another form of cultural analysis. Thus, the articles by Gillison and Poole show how, in two New Guinea Highlands societies, cannibal customs are richly enmeshed with elements of ritual and myth and with convoluted notions pertaining to the human body. Sahlins takes masterful advantage of the extensive historical documentation on Fiji, blending this with his own empirical findings, to produce a major statement on the place of cannibalism in the culture of these islands. MacCormack likewise combines historical and ethnographic materials drawn from a West African society, thus developing an analysis of the symbolic and political implications of cannibalistic belief, and of the role of cannibal accusation in Sherbro politics. Tuzin examines the psychocultural factors influencing the puzzling response of the Arapesh of lowland New Guinea to the event of Japanese cannibal predation during World War II.

All of the essays originated in a symposium, "The Ethnography of Cannibalism," sponsored by the American Anthropological Association and convened in Washington, D.C., in December 1980. The authors and editors are grateful to Professor Shirley Lindenbaum for her illuminating commentary on the symposium and for contributing her expanded remarks as a fitting conclusion to the published collection.

DONALD TUZIN
PAULA BROWN

REFERENCES

ANTHROPOLOGICAL INSTITUTE OF GREAT BRITAIN AND IRELAND. 1892 *Notes and Queries on Anthropology* (2nd ed.). (John George Garson and Charles Hercules Read, eds.) London: The Anthropological Institute.
ARENS, WILLIAM. 1979. *The Man-Eating Myth: Anthropology and Anthropophagy*. London: Oxford University Press.

DORNSTREICH, M. D., and G. E. B. MORREN. 1974. Does New Guinea Cannibalism Have Nutritional Value? *Human Ecology* 2:1–12.

GAJDUSEK, D. C. 1977. The Unconventional Viruses and the Origin and Disappearance of Kuru. *Science* 197:943–960.

HARNER, MICHAEL. 1977. The Ecological Basis for Aztec Sacrifice. *American Ethnologist* 4:117–135.

HERODOTUS. 1952. *The History*. (George Rawlinson, trans.) Chicago: Encyclopaedia Britannica. (Original ca. 450 B.C.)

HARRIS, MARVIN. 1977. *Cannibals and Kings*. New York: Random House.

LINDENBAUM, SHIRLEY. 1979. *Kuru Sorcery: Disease and Danger in the New Guinea Highlands*. Palo Alto, Calif.: Mayfield.

SAGAN, ELI. 1974. *Cannibalism: Human Aggression and Cultural Form*. New York: Harper & Row.

Cannibals, Tricksters, and Witches

Anthropophagic Images Among Bimin-Kuskusmin

FITZ JOHN PORTER POOLE

INTRODUCTION

In this essay I explore selected features of the cultural construction of cannibalism among the Bimin-Kuskusmin of the West Sepik interior of Papua New Guinea. A recent debate has challenged the authenticity of ethnographic accounts of putatively witnessed, customary cannibalism (see Arens 1979; cf. Rivière 1980). Although I note all observed instances of anthropophagy as custom, I do not intend to enter into this controversy here. Whether or not cannibalism actually does occur, the problem of analysis involves at least an interpretation of the symbolic, metaphoric, or ideological dimensions of the reported acts or beliefs. Thus, this analysis is concerned with a

FITZ JOHN PORTER POOLE is Assistant Professor of Anthropology at the University of California, San Diego.

Field research was supported by the National Institutes of Health, the Cornell University Humanities and Social Sciences Program, and the Center for South Pacific Studies of the University of California, Santa Cruz. An earlier version of this paper was presented at the 79th Annual Meeting of the American Anthropological Association in Washington, D.C. For critical comments on the presented version, I thank P. Brown, G. H. Herdt, S. Lindenbaum, T. Moylan, R. I. Rosaldo, Jr., M. D. Sahlins, and D. F. Tuzin.

cultural interpretation of ideas of anthropophagy, and focuses on several interrelated contexts in which Bimin-Kuskusmin perceptions of cannibalism are articulated. First, I plot the major contours of the Bimin-Kuskusmin cultural map of a regional landscape of anthropophagic beings and practices. Second, I examine particular aspects of cannibalism within Bimin-Kuskusmin society in terms of cultural images of sorcerers, tricksters, and witches, and of social acts of funerary and warfare cannibalism. Third, I draw together these several themes in analyzing the "great pandanus rite" *(seair ben aiyem ser)*.[1] Indeed, in a highly condensed and symbolically elaborate manner, the major dimensions of Bimin-Kuskusmin cannibalism are represented and illuminated in the ethnographic context of this ritual performance.

A LANDSCAPE OF CANNIBALS

Bimin-Kuskusmin interpret the significance of the anthropophagy of other ethnic groups in terms of their own cannibalistic beliefs and practices. Thus, they maintain that for the nearby Miyanmin, whom they regard with fear and horror as the regional cannibals par excellence, the search for human flesh is an end in itself (cf. Dornstreich and Morren 1974:6). But they admit that they have never witnessed more than Miyanmin warriors bearing human bodies away from the Telefolmin plateau after raids. Bimin-Kuskusmin contrast Miyanmin anthropophagic practice, nevertheless, with *their own.* For Miyanmin, they claim, humans indeed do become food in an ordinary sense and are seen as comparable to pigs and marsupials. Miyanmin eat human bodies *in toto* and with little sense of ceremony and etiquette, which are held to be signs of true barbarism. In contrast, Bimin-Kuskusmin reject the view that any parts of human bodies can become "food" *(yemen)* in any ordinary sense. They do acknowledge, however, that the restricted consumption of certain parts of certain persons by particular social others in special

---

[1] This complex rite, which reportedly occurred only once every several decades, was never witnessed, and all data concerning the performance were reconstructed from independent interviews with several ritual elders. Both skeletal and other *sacrae* that are said to be part of this ritual, however, were indeed present at the recognized site of the great pandanus rite. The last performance may have occurred in the middle to late 1940s.

contexts and in a prescribed manner is of major ritual importance. And the complex symbolism that marks these contexts, beliefs, and acts is densely articulated with other realms of Bimin-Kuskusmin cultural construction and social action.

Almost one thousand Bimin-Kuskusmin dwell in a rugged, ecologically diverse, mountainous area of the southeastern Telefolmin District of the West Sepik Province of Papua New Guinea. Speaking a Mountain-Ok language, they note with pride an historical sense of their unique cultural traditions and areal impor- tance, and they emphasize a complex ritual legacy as being central to their identity (see Poole 1976, 1981b, 1982). What they consider to be unique forms of cannibalism characterize aspects of this ritual heritage and distinguish the perceived nature of Bimin-Kuskusmin anthropophagy from that of all other known groups of the Mountain-Ok area. But networks of trade, alliance, warfare, inter- marriage, and ritual relations bring them into some manner of con- tact with other ethnic groups of the Mountain-Ok region and beyond (see Barth 1971, 1975; Brumbaugh 1980; Poole 1976; Stead- man 1975). All of these ethnic groups are believed to practice some forms of cannibalism. Ethnic maps of regional anthropophagic practice, however, appear to differ markedly. For example, the neighboring Oksapmin apparently claim that neither they nor the Bimin-Kuskusmin engage in cannibalistic acts of any kind (T. Moylan, personal communication).

Bimin-Kuskusmin traditionally partition all known ethnic groups into four concentric zones of beings, and different modes of an- thropophagy are among the distinctive features that define each zone. From the center to the periphery of the traditionally known world, these zones are: "true men" (kunum fen); "human men" (kunum kaptiip); "human creatures" (kaptiip); and "animal-man beings" (samaar kunum kaptiip). Within the central zone, which originally encompassed only Bimin-Kuskusmin,[2] considerations of the gender, the kinship relations, and the ritual status of both living and dead persons mark all aspects of cannibalism in contexts of mortuary rites and warfare. In addition, a complex reckoning of

---

[2] With the advent of the *Pax Australiana* and increasing intergroup contact, by 1971 this central zone had come to include other nearby groups and the more distant Telefolmin for certain purposes of ethnic classification.

male and female anatomical parts of human bodies governs notions about what kinds flesh may be properly consumed by particular persons in certain anthropophagic acts. The cannibalistic consumption of male parts of either male or female corpses is believed to strengthen the hard, strong, internal, ritually significant "male anatomy" of either men or women. Such acts also weaken the soft, weak, external, ritually unimportant "female anatomy" of persons of either sex. Conversely, the anthropophagic consumption of female parts weakens the "male anatomy" and strengthens the "female anatomy." Similarly, male or female foods strengthen male or female parts of the anatomy of humans, respectively, although human substance is never classified as food.

Among Bimin-Kuskusmin, anthropophagic acts that do not take account of matters of gender, kinship, ritual status, and bodily substance in ritually prescribed ways are held to be signs of desperation, derangement, or denial of the moral and jural attributes and capacities of full personhood and true humanity. Thus, the cannibalistic practices of socially and culturally distant groups are often viewed as barbaric and inhuman. Similarly, the anthropophagic impulses of the insane, the possessed, the morally flawed, and the starving, as well as forest demons, sorcerers, tricksters, witches, and even women and children,[3] are believed to be beyond the pale of moral and jural order and control. Such beings ignore or deliberately violate the ritual rules of appropriate cannibalism, and they are contemplated by Bimin-Kuskusmin with horror and disgust.[4]

Somewhat familiar, but less constrained anthropophagic prac-

---

[3] Denied the strengthening qualities of male initiation rites and ritually significant male foods, both women and children are often said to be overcome by uncontrollable rage and hunger for human flesh and to take cannibalistic revenge against others. Such fantasies are often articulated in the images of female witches who devour male substance, or of unborn or unweaned, but omnivorous infants who attack and consume the womb and later the nipple. In fact, children are forbidden to engage in any cannibalistic acts, and certain anthropophagic practices are prescribed only for menstruous, initiated women or for female ritual elders in restricted ritual contexts (usually mortuary rites).

[4] Many Bimin-Kuskusmin men and women whom I interviewed and who admitted to socially proper cannibalistic practices acknowledged considerable ambivalence, horror, and disgust at their own acts. Many persons noted that they had been unable to engage in the act, had not completed it, had vomited or even fainted, or had hidden the prescribed morsel and had lied about consuming it. One might suspect that some expressions of disgust were shaped by the knowledge that Europeans (government officers and missionaries) were strongly against such practices. But in the acts of funerary cannibalism that I did witness on eleven occasions, such extreme reticence and ambivalence were frequently noted.

tices are recognized within the surrounding zone of human men, which is a region that is known from experience. This zone encompasses those groups with which the Bimin-Kuskusmin interact directly on a more or less regular basis, and which form a "buffer zone" between Bimin-Kuskusmin and the horrors of the human creatures and animal-man beings that are to be found beyond. Indeed, the human men must fight continually with the human creatures, and such warfare involves far more frequent and indiscriminate cannibalism than Bimin-Kuskusmin inflict upon human men. It is within the zone of human men, however, that those groups with which Bimin-Kuskusmin trade, ally themselves, fight, intermarry, and forge ritual relations are to be found. Despite recognized interethnic differences among groups of human men, Bimin-Kuskusmin acknowledge a common ground of similarity in moral values, jural order, and ritual endeavors. And ties of friendship, kinship, and marriage also facilitate sustained interactions with some of these groups. But from among these nearby groups come those particular communities that are the source of the dreaded *tamam* witchcraft (see Poole 1981a), and that are perceived at some particular historical moment as "major strong enemies" *(maraak duur ser)*. Witches commit illicit acts of cannibalism against Bimin-Kuskusmin by stealth and wile. Major enemies confront each other, however, with anthropophagic atrocities on the field of battle.

The human men are said to devour large quantities of both male and female parts of Bimin-Kuskusmin warriors slain in major battles, as well as of women and children killed in hamlet raids. This unrestrained cannibalism is believed to be a desperate attempt to gain some of the famed ritual prowess of the Bimin-Kuskusmin through indiscriminate consumption of their bodily substance. It is said that in the past, groups of human men would even steal the corpses of Bimin-Kuskusmin from burial platforms for similar purposes. However, Bimin-Kuskusmin warriors would consume only small morsels of the female parts of slain human *men*—and never women, children, or burial cadavers—as an act of contempt, for the Bimin-Kuskusmin do not value the ritual strength of the bodily substance of these beings under most circumstances. But there is one remarkable exception. From one of these major enemy groups—an Oksapmin settlement in the southeastern Bak valley to the north—the Bimin-Kuskusmin claim to have captured their sacrificial victims (male and female) for the great pandanus rite. This ritual performance, however, transformed the social identity of the Oksapmin victims in complex ways.

In the third zone, the human creatures reign. These peoples are beyond the range of Bimin-Kuskusmin social interaction, but they are said to have regular contact with groups that are known directly to the Bimin-Kuskusmin. On occasion, they have been sighted from afar, and tales recount the wanderings of lone Bimin-Kuskusmin men who have been lost to them. The human creatures are reputed to be ferocious in war and prone to cannibalistic excesses. They consider human beings to be ordinary food, to be combined with pork and other animal and vegetable foods in vast earth ovens. Men, women, and even children participate eagerly and indiscriminately in such feasts, and their settlements are said to be perpetually littered with dismembered human remains. Removing only the gall bladder, which fouls the taste of human flesh, they eat all other parts of their victims. And, in rites of incestuous copulation, they devour the severed gall bladders. They do not discriminate in any way between the dead of other groups and their own dead. Indeed, it is said that they will kill their own kith and kin in minor disputes and eat their bodies without the slightest ceremony. Critical differences of gender, kinship, ritual status, and bodily substance are of no consequence to them. They engage in warfare as an incessant search for human food, and they are known to carry large numbers of trussed bodies from distant battlefields to their own villages. Some unfortunate Bimin-Kuskusmin, who were visiting friends, kin, or affines abroad, are known to have been captured and eaten by them, and they are greatly feared in a way more tangible than that felt for the mythic animal-man beings beyond them. The infamous Miyanmin are often cited as the most terrifying example of such human creatures, who conduct deliberately cannibalistic raids against major enemies of the Bimin-Kuskusmin in the zone of human men. Although these major enemies cannot successfully defend themselves against the horrifying attacks of human creatures and often seek revenge among nearby groups (e.g., among Bimin-Kuskusmin), the fearsome human creatures themselves fall prey to the ravages of the dreaded animal-man beings.

If Bimin-Kuskusmin classify themselves as true men, bound to a proper moral and jural order and to ritually sanctioned modes of anthropophagy, then their antithesis is to be found at the periphery of the known world and beyond, in the form of animal-man beings. These deformed monsters, who possess few vestiges of moral and social responsibility, are renowned for heinous acts of indiscriminate cannibalism, incest, and murder. They are said to eat their firstborn children at whim and even to gnaw on their own limbs.[5] Groups of men or women hide in the forest to capture members of the opposite sex and then to sever and consume their genitalia whole. Men are said to rip unborn infants from the wombs of pregnant women, who sometimes eat their own aborted young. Unwary travelers who fall prey to their lust for blood and flesh may be eaten alive, for they are known to delight in torture. Without the implements of hunting and trapping, their only meat is human. Without fire, they must eat their fare raw. They leave no bodily parts untouched and even pound the remaining bones into an edible mush. They especially prize brains, intestinal feces, and gall bladders, which Bimin-Kuskusmin consider to be repugnant in the extreme. It is said that on occasion, in the distant past, some young Bimin-Kuskusmin men may have wandered abroad and never returned, perhaps having passed into the territory of the animal-man beings to be hideously devoured.

Of course, these animal-man monsters are believed to be far beyond the pale of any ordinary social interaction, and they are portrayed largely in tales that are told at night around the flickering hearth fires to frighten unruly children. But these young children, often no more than four or five years of age, may project these fearful images on parental figures, whom they have already come to view as anxiety-provoking "monsters" of another kind, when they learn of their own parents' cannibalistic acts for the first time. These youngsters were already at an age when parent-child tensions are high. Having witnessed their parents' mortuary anthropophagy, many of these children suddenly avoided their parents, shrieked in their presence, or expressed unusual fear of them. After such ex-

---

[5] As a mythic prelude to the advent of death, some perverted early ancestors are said to have eaten their firstborn and to have used their skins to cover drums that were major *sacrae* of salt-making rites. When these cannibalistic acts were seen to have brought mortality to Bimin-Kuskusmin, these ancestors were banished to the outermost zone of animal-man beings.

periences, several children recounted dreams or constructed fantasies about animal-man beings with the faces or other features of particular parents who were smeared with blood and organs.

IMAGES AND ACTS OF BIMIN-KUSKUSMIN CANNIBALISM

Although these zones of beings provide an idiom for distinguishing Bimin-Kuskusmin cannibalism from other recognized kinds, the special characteristics of Bimin-Kuskusmin anthropophagy are most often elaborated in the images of sorcerers, tricksters, and witches, and in particular acts of mortuary rites and of warfare. Indeed, all of these cultural constructions of cannibalism are implicated in the symbolism of the great pandanus rite.

Although sorcerers, tricksters, and witches are all cannibals, the ideal victims of both sorcerers and tricksters are *tamam* witches, who attack ordinary humans (see Poole 1981a). Female sorcerers are known to consume only the most polluting of female bodily substances, which they transform into ritually powerful male substances. They effect this mystical transformation by using male ritual *sacrae* to ward off pollution and to enhance the male strength of their own bodies. In this regard, they are the antithesis of female *tamam* witches, who use perversions of male ritual *sacrae* to convert male into female substance. The *tamam* witch is grossly fat in her excess of female substance, and she is often barren or only capable of bearing monsters.[6] In contrast, the *büs* or *kümon* female sorcerer is lean in her bodily emphasis on strong male substance, and she is known to be very fertile and a mother of many sons. The female sorcerer effectively destroys *tamam* witches (both female and male) through cannibalism of their female parts, which are the basis of witchcraft capacity.

Male *büs* and *kümon* sorcerers, however, are reputed to eat both powerful male and polluted female bodily substances and to strengthen the strong male parts of the bodies of both their victims and themselves by such cannablistic acts. Male sorcerers, who are more powerful than their female counterparts, are also the anti-

---

[6] Although *tamam* witches may be either male or female in appearance, their essential bodily and spiritual characteristics mark them as being female in their basic nature.

thesis of female *tamam* witches, who are more deadly than male witches. The female witch eats and transforms male substance, which she ritually pollutes, into "naturally" polluted female substance and destroys the ritual importance of the "male anatomy." But male witches are said to consume various aspects of both the female and the male substance of their victims. They do not transform female into male substance or vice versa. Instead, they are known to neutralize the polluting, strengthening, reproductive, and ritual qualities of both female and male bodily substances and to render them ineffectual and harmless. In contrast, the male sorcerer devours both male and female substance, but transforms the latter into the former in order to ensure the efficacy of ritual endeavors, fertility, propagation, and growth as they affect both humans and ritually significant crops and game. Male sorcerers often cooperate with female ritual elders in the killing of *tamam* witches, but the sorcerers destroy witches by the anthropophagic consumption of all polluted bodily substances, which they transform and either strengthen (as male substances) or destroy (as female substances). Female elders do not use cannibalism against witches (see Poole 1981b).

The image of the trickster also has male and female manifestations. The female trickster *(kamdaak waneng)* is believed to consume female substance both in the bodies of men and in her own body. She destroys male witches. In many tales of tricksters, she is portrayed as possessing the uncanny ability to use the female substance that she has eaten to transform herself into a powerful male ritual leader who performs wondrous feats. Both by consuming her own female parts and by performing male ritual acts, she is able to overcome her female appearance and polluting legacy to achieve a thoroughly masculine identity in body, spirit, and behavior. But her female identity soon reappears.

In contrast, the male trickster *gabruurian* is known to eat contaminated male substance both in the bodies of women and in his own body. He devours female witches. In several tales, he is shown to possess the remarkable capacity to use the polluted male substance that he has devoured to transform himself into an androgynous female ritual elder who is ritually powerful and free of pollution (see Poole 1981b). As a consequence of this new identity, the trickster *gabruurian* is able to kill and to eat both male and female witches in ways that are similar to those of female ritual elders who, however, do not eat witches. Yet, the severe pollution that is produced by these cannibalistic acts transforms *gabruurian* once again into a male figure.[7]

Beyond these cultural images of extraordinary cannibals, there are those anthropophagic acts of ordinary adult Bimin-Kuskusmin that are bound up with warfare and funerals. On the field of battle, only fully initiated men may consume certain female parts (e.g., flesh and fat, but not muscle, of thighs and upper arms) of slain warriors of other ethnic groups who are not kin, close affines, or ritual leaders.[8] The bodies are dismembered, and the heads are severed and buried. The bodily parts are eaten raw. Only major enemy groups are the focus of warfare cannibalism. Such defilement is believed to preclude proper funerals and ancestorhood for the enemy dead, and the bodily parts that are consumed emphasize the weak, female character of the fallen warriors in an expression of deliberate contempt. Women do not participate in such war-related cannibalism, nor do male ritual elders defile enemy bodies in the normal course of events.[9]

All *observed* instances of Bimin-Kuskusmin anthropophagy, however, are *customary* aspects of mortuary rites. Male lineage agnates of a deceased, initiated man, but not his direct descendants, should eat morsels of his bone marrow (male substance).[10] I have witnessed this act on five occasions. Such cannibalism is believed to honor the deceased, to counteract the extreme pollution of his mor-

---

[7] Under most circumstances, female pollution is believed to weaken male characteristics and to strengthen female traits. In the case of tricksters, however, this and other aspects of the normal order are reversed in often bizarre ways.

[8] Although I have never observed such acts, two such events reportedly occurred during field research; and 87 men discussed their own participation in war-related cannibalism.

[9] When new shields are being consecrated for placement in war cult houses, hearts of renowned enemy warriors are said to be taken for purposes of the ritual sanctification of these shields. The heart is bisected, and one half is fastened to the center of the new shield with a ritual war arrow. The other half is again bisected. One portion is sacrificed to appropriate ancestors inside of a dog skull, and male ritual elders consume the other portion. This act is said both to defile the dead and to draw their ritual power into the Bimin-Kuskusmin war cult. I have seen the sacrifice of an enemy heart, as well as a rotting heart on a recently consecrated shield, but I have not witnessed the associated anthropophagic act.

[10] Because of a special bond of substance between them, parents and children (or other direct descendants) may not consume parts of each other in funerals, engage in sexual intercourse with each other, or accept death compensation for each other.

tuary rites, to ensure the safe passage of his *finiik* spirit to the ancestral underworld, and to "recycle" his procreative and ritual strength within his patrilineage. His female lineage agnates, however, eat small morsels of his lower belly fat (female substance). I have observed this event four times. This anthropophagic practice is believed to enhance female reproductive and ritual power through the consumption of female substance that has been in prolonged contact with strong male substance, that is, genital parts that have endured the ordeals of male initiation and have powerful procreative functions. The wife of a deceased man, if she is still within her childbearing years, is expected to eat a tiny, raw fragment of flesh from her dead husband's penis. I have twice seen a dead man's penis flesh presented to his widow, but I have never clearly witnessed its consumption. Indeed, most Bimin-Kuskusmin consider this mortuary act to be particularly degrading and disgusting, and they claim that women often hide or vomit these morsels. This form of cannibalism is said to enhance a woman's fertility and to bind her reproductive capacity to her deceased husband's living agnates.[11]

It is also customary among Bimin-Kuskusmin that male lineage agnates of a deceased, initiated woman should eat fragments of her bone marrow to honor her reproductive capacity, which is associated with male bodily substance. I have observed this act on three occasions. This form of anthropophagy is intended to perpetuate her procreative powers among the living women and even inmarried wives of her patrilineage and to offset the considerable pollution of her funerary rites. In this manner, her male lineage agnates are said to reclaim her reproductive capacity from her husband's lineage and clan agnates, for whom she bore children. Her female lineage agnates and sometimes female cognatic kin, however, eat morsels of her lower belly fat. I have seen five instances of this form of mortuary cannibalism. This practice is believed to enhance and to perpetuate the deceased woman's reproductive power, which is highly concentrated in her abdomen at the moment of her death, among the women of her lineage and sometimes of her kindred. The husband of a deceased woman, if he is still sexually and ritually active, is obliged to eat a small, raw fragment of flesh from his dead

---

[11] Widow remarriage and the preferred levirate are ideally practiced within the lineage and often within the clan.

wife's vagina. I have witnessed four events of this kind. This act of cannibalism is said to enhance the reproductive capacity of the man's daughters who were born to the dead wife and to protect him against the attacks of *tamam* witches. The husband is extraordinarily polluted, nevertheless, by this mortuary performance, and he is required to undergo extensive purificatory rites in seclusion.

When paramount ritual elders of a clan die, their agnatic lineage kin participate in the same cannibalistic acts as those that are prescribed for the funerals of ordinary adult men and women; but spouses of the deceased elders may not engage in mortuary anthropophagy. At the funerals of paramount male ritual elders, other male elders of the clan eat parts of the deceased's raw heart tissue. I have observed this practice on two occasions. This form of anthropophagy is believed to ensure that the great ritural power and knowledge of the dead man is perpetuated in the ritual elders of his clan through the consumption of one of the most ritually significant and powerful male parts of the anatomy.[12] At the death of paramount female ritual elders, however, other female elders of the clan and female uterine kin consume morsels of the dead woman's uterus and interior parts of the vagina. I have witnessed this act only once. Such cannibalism is said to ensure that the ritual power of the deceased is perpetuated among the female ritual elders of her clan, and that her reproductive power (without the pollution of menstrual capacity) is diffused among her uterine kin. In this context, both ritual and reproductive power are associated with female substance (i.e., uterus and vagina), but this form of female substance has been purified and strengthened by special rites of initiation for paramount female elders (see Poole 1981b).

THE GREAT PANDANUS RITE

Aspects of the symbolism of all of the cultural constructions of cannibalism mentioned above are incorporated in performances of the great pandanus rite. About once every generation, the great

---

[12] The mystical efficacy of male ritual, food, experience, and knowledge is believed to have a profound affect on the heart, which is the vital center of emotion, intellect, mystical power, judgmental capacity, and moral and jural responsibility for Bimin-Kuskusmin.

pandanus rite is said to have been held in a sacred grove of giant pandanus trees near the western end of the northern Bimin-Kuskusmin valley. This grove is set apart as a major ritual site, and pandanus nuts are harvested there only for ritual purposes. Many shrines, ritual boundary markers, and other *sacrae* mark this carefully tended clearing. The decorated skulls that are bound to the upper trunks of the pandanus trees and the great log platforms that bridge the span between some of these trees bear witness to details of the great pandanus rite as ritual elders describe it.

Reconstruction of the event suggests that it encompassed two performances. Each phase of the long, elaborate drama of the rite lasted about ten days and ideally involved the active participation of all adult, fully initiated men and women of the Bimin-Kuskusmin. The first performance was held roughly in September or October at the beginning of a major, semiannual harvest of nut pandanus. This phase of the rite was focused on the fertility, propagation, and growth of the *kauun* nut pandanus, which is a semidomesticated crop and a "female food" *(yemen yangus),* and it required an adult male victim. The second phase took place approximately in May or June at the end of the other semiannual pandanus harvest. This ritual performance was focused on the fertility, propagation, and growth of the *bokhuur* nut pandanus, which is a wild crop and a "male food" *(yemen imok),* and it required an adult female victim. In each phase, complex acts of ritual cannibalism by both men and women were central to the performance. And these anthropophagic acts were bound up with the sacrifice and consumption of male or female parts of cassowaries and wild boars, which are said to be involved in the "natural" propagation of *kauun* and *bokhuur* pandanus and are believed to be endowed with attributes of human personhood. Throughout both ritual phases, there was an elaborate symmetry and complementarity in regard to relationships between male and female victims, anatomical parts, foods, and ritual participants. Prior to each performance, Bimin-Kuskusmin ritual elders launched raiding expeditions to capture an appropriate victim from the prescribed Oksapmin community of human men, and hunters were sent into the deep forest in search of cassowaries and wild boars.

In the first performance, a massive log was lashed between the upper trunks of two *kauun* pandanus trees, which are classified as female trees. At the ends of the log, the skulls of male victims from previous performances were bound, cleaned, and redecorated with red pigment and ceremonial headdresses that displayed red Raggiana bird of paradise plumes, cassowary feathers, and wild boar bristles.[13] These ritual emblems are identical to those that adorn the skulls of paramount male ritual elders at the conclusion of their mortuary rites. The hunters, who intoned the death chants of their clans, brought the freshly killed cassowaries and wild boars from the forest to the ritual clearing. Ritual elders butchered the carcasses and retained only the strong, hard, internal, and ritually significant male parts of the cassowaries (primarily hearts, bone marrow, and genitalia) and only the weak, soft, external, and ritually unimportant female parts of the boars (primarily lower belly fat). All other parts of these creatures were sacrificed to the "great ancestors" *(khyrkhymin ser)* of all Bimin-Kuskusmin.[14] The remaining parts of the cassowaries and wild boars then were steamed with taro, which is a male food par excellence, in a ritual earth oven. Children were warned not to approach the sacred grove, and smoke began to pour from the sacrificial fires of myriad clan cult houses throughout Bimin-Kuskusmin territory. A central rite of fertility for both pandanus crops and humans was about to begin.

When the raiders returned from Oksapmin territory with their live male victim, he was bound to the center of the great log on his back, with his face upward. He was dressed in the regalia of a Bimin-Kuskusmin paramount male ritual elder. He was fed on strong male foods and guarded throughout the night. But at dawn on the following day, arrows were driven into his thighs and upper arms, and bone slivers were inserted in strategic areas of his torso from the groin to upper chest. The special arrows, which are implements of war, marked those female parts of a major enemy that are deemed proper for cannibalistic consumption by initiated Bimin-

---

[13] In this ritual context, red is symbolic of male substance. This association is drawn from the essential red color of "agnatic blood" *(kunum khaim)*.

[14] These great ancestors are believed to participate in the consumption of sacrificial victims, both human and nonhuman, and to devour bodily parts of human cadavers on burial platforms in order to quicken the decomposition of the corpse and the passage of the *finiik* spirit of the deceased to the ancestral underworld. In contrast, ghosts of the recently dead may take capricious cannibalistic revenge upon the living for real and imagined insults and injuries.

Kuskusmin men. The pattern of bone slivers, however, indicated a stereotypic mode of killing *tamam* witches by sorcerers or ritual experts (see Pool 1981a). And the origin of *tamam* witchcraft is attributed to certain groups of Oksapmin, including the prescribed community of the victim, who are major enemies.

It is said that ideally the victim should not have died until dusk, and some effort was made to prolong his agony but to ensure that he did not die prematurely. Both the trauma and the duration of the victim's dying are believed to have strengthened his male substance and, therefore, to have enhanced the efficacy of the great pandanus rite. Once he was dead, however, his corpse was lowered to the ground, and female ritual elders began to butcher the body. The head, which was decorated with red pigment and the headdress of a male ritual elder, was severed and tied to one of the *kauun* pandanus trees to rot. The heat and fumes of the decaying head are said to have increased the sacredness and fertility of the *kauun* tree. The gall bladder, which is believed to contaminate and foul human flesh, was removed and discarded. Finally, various ritually prescribed portions of the dismembered cadaver were distributed by the female ritual elders to different categories of participants in the rite. The remaining, proscribed anatomical parts were placed around the base of the *kauun* tree that did not hold the severed head of the victim. The symbolic juxtaposition of the elevated, severed head (male substance in both ritual and "natural" terms) and the lower, discarded bodily parts (largely female substance in "natural" terms) in relation to the *kauun* trees and the sacrificial log is said to have ensured that the fertility of the pandanus trees would provide abundant harvests for years to come. These ritual insignia of bodily substance marked the trees as being male (with male substance) and female (with female substance), and the sacrificial log was designated as a phallus in the accompanying ritual chants. But acts of ritual anthropophagy were considered also to be necesary for the desired efficacy of the great pandanus rite to be fulfilled.

The fat and flesh of the victim's thighs and upper arms (female substance) were distributed at once to all initiated men who were not ritual elders. Small morsels were quickly roasted after being steamed and then were eaten, and all initiated men of ordinary status were expected to participate in this act. This cannibalistic deed was seen as a defilement of the headless corpse of a male major enemy by initiated Bimin-Kuskusmin warriors. Its symbolism drew upon more ordinary acts of war-related cannibalism. In the context of the great pandanus rite, however, such anthropophagic defilement by the eating of roasted (not raw) morsels of female substance is said to have diminished the major enemy status of the victim, who thereafter would be treated as a deceased Bimin-Kuskusmin man in at least some respects. The initiated men who consumed these bodily parts, both on the battlefield (raw) and in the great pandanus rite (roasted and steamed), became highly polluted and polluting, and they immediately ate male parts (bone marrow) of cassowaries to offset this contamination. The significance of this act is linked to the funerary cannibalism of a deceased man's male lineage agnates. But in the great pandanus rite, the consumption of cassowary bone marrow, which is an exceptionally powerful male substance, is believed to have enhanced the fertility of both humans (through men's subsequent procreative acts) and pandanus trees (through men's present ritual acts).

The heart and genitalia of the victim (male substance) were presented to male and female ritual elders, respectively, to eat raw. These cannibalistic acts were performed in explicit recognition of the ritual and social Bimin-Kuskusmin identity that had been conferred upon the victim in the great pandanus rite through a sacrificial death and bodily decoration. The eating of the victim's heart by male elders is believed to be somewhat analogous to the mortuary cannibalism in which such elders participate at the funerals of the paramount male ritual leaders of their clans. In the great pandanus rite, however, the ritual strength that was transferred to the victim through ritual adornment, sacrifice, and endurance of a slow and painful death is said to have been incorporated in all male ritual elders of the Bimin-Kuskusmin by their collective cannibalistic consumption of the single victim's heart. These same male elders then reinforced the efficacy of this anthropophagic act by eating cooked portions of cassowary hearts, which are among the most powerful of male substances in all ritual contexts.

The consumption of the victim's genitalia by female elders, however, is an act that draws symbolic significance from the mortuary cannibalism of a deceased man's wife. In this funerary form of anthropophagy, both the dead man and his still fertile widow are viewed as ordinary, adult, initiated Bimin-Kuskusmin. But in the great pandanus rite, the female ritual elders who ate parts of the victim's genitalia were postmenopausal, androgynous, and past their reproductive years (see Poole 1981b). The victim, who came from the Oksapmin source of *tamam* witchcraft, was seen somewhat ambivalently as possessing the procreative power of an initiated man and the ritual power of both a male elder (by ritual endowment in the great pandanus rite) and a *tamam* witch (by "natural" endowment at birth). It is the Bimin-Kuskusmin female ritual elder who is the witch-hunter par excellence, and she often employs the occult techniques of the female *tamam* witch through the voracious, destructive consumption of male substance to destroy powers of witchcraft. In this ritual context, she is said to have obliterated the innate witchcraft capacity of the victim by ripping, tearing, and eating his male substance in the form of his penis. In so doing, she removed a dangerous source of pollution from a major rite that was focused on matters of fertility, propagation, and growth, and she temporarily rid the wider Bimin-Kuskusmin community of the threat of witchcraft attacks, which can cause illness, barrenness, and death.

The female ritual elder is also believed to have harnessed the male reproductive and ritual power of the victim to her own androgynous ritual power through this cannibalistic act. Her ability to ensure fertility, propagation, and growth in pregnancy rites, birth rituals, and children's rites of passage was enhanced by this male substance. But the consumption of the victim's genitalia was also highly polluting to the female elders, who promptly ate parts of the androgynous genitalia of cassowaries to counteract this severe contamination. Both the female elder and the cassowary, who are representations of the hermaphroditic ancestor of all Bimin-Kuskusmin, Afek, are similar with respect to their androgynous natures. Thus, the ambiguous character of the cassowary's genitalia is perceived to have been an appropriate antidote to the polluting effects of consuming the genitalia of the victim, who was cast in the images of both a dangerous male enemy and a polluting female witch.

The ritual destruction of the victim's witchcraft capacity and enhancement of his reproductive and ritual power for the fertility of humans and pandanus trees, however, required further reduction of his polluting female substance through cannibalistic acts. Both men and women were expected to consume *all* of the victim's lower belly fat, which is an especially contaminating part of the "female anatomy." The Bimin-Kuskusmin women who participated in this aspect of the rite were explicitly linked to several distinct female images of anthropophagy in elaborate ritual oratory. The first image was associated with the cannibalistic consumption of a deceased man's lower belly fat by his female lineage agnates, who gain reproductive and ritual power through his substance in this customary funerary act. In the great pandanus rite, however, analogous forms of anthropophagy are believed not only to have promoted female ritual power and fertility for both humans and pandanus trees, but also to have reduced dangerous substances in the victim's body that might have interfered with fertility in both ritual and "natural" terms. The second image was that of the witch-killing female sorcerer. Some women carried the characteristic male ritual implements and *sacrae* of sorcerers as they proceeded to eat the victim's lower belly fat. Indeed, before consuming their allotted morsels, these women used male ritual mortars and pestles to grind the fat into a jelly-like substance. The third image drew upon the transformative powers of the female trickster *kamdaak waneng*. Several women wore the odd, male regalia of *kamdaak waneng* and slashed their abdomens, thighs, and upper arms with male ritual knives. They are perceived as having been especially instrumental in transforming the identity of the sacrificial victim from that of a *tamam* witch, who possessed exaggerated female characteristics, to that of a paramount male ritual elder, who possessed powerful masculine traits and ritual strength.

Although women participants predominated in these aspects of the great pandanus rite, men too, as ritual impersonators of sorcerers and witches, lessened the victim's dangerous witchcraft capability by eating his female substance. Both men and women were expected to reinforce the ritual efficacy of these anthropophagic acts by also consuming the lower belly fat of wild boars. Through their collective contribution to the ritual transformation of the victim's identity and the consequent efficacy of the rite, however, both men and women experienced severe pollution in different ways. The male participants became contaminated and weakened their male substance by eating the highly polluted substance of a *tamam* witch, although the victim was male. The female participants became polluted and damaged their female substance by devouring the ritually powerful substance of a wild boar, although the parts consumed were female. In both cases, these ritual performers were required to undergo rites of purification and subsequent divination to ensure that the bodily and spiritual balances of their appropriate gender had been restored.

In the second performance of the great pandanus rite, another great log was bound between the upper trunks of two *bokhuur* pandanus trees, which are classified as male trees. At each end of this log, the skulls of female victims from prior performances were fastened, scrubbed, and once again adorned with black pigment and ritual headdresses that exhibited black cockatoo feathers, cassowary plumes, and wild boar bristles.[15] These ceremonial insignia are identical to those that decorate the skulls of paramount female ritual elders at the end of their funerary rites. Once again, hunters carried newly slaughtered cassowaries and wild boars to the ritual site. Again, ritual elders butchered the carcasses. But in this performance, they retained only the weak, soft, external, and ritually insignificant female parts of the cassowaries (primarily lower belly fat) and only the strong, hard, internal, and ritually important male parts of the boars (primarily hearts, bone marrow, and genitalia). Once again, all other parts of these creatures were sacrificed to the great ancestors of all Bimin-Kuskusmin. The remaining parts of the cassowaries and wild boars then were steamed with sweet potato, which is a female food of major importance, in the earth oven. Again, children were excluded from the sacred grove, and the clan cult houses became ritually active in preparation for the second phase of the great pandanus rite.

When the warriors brought back their live female victim from the Oksapmin, she was lashed to the center of the massive log on her side and with her face downward. She was adorned in the manner of a Bimin-Kuskusmin paramount female ritual elder. She was fed exclusively female foods and tended throughout the night. But at dawn on the following day, she too was impaled with arrows in her thighs and upper arms and with bone slivers in her upper torso. Once again, the ritual emblems of a major enemy and a *tamam* witch symbolically identified the victim. Again, the victim lingered in her death throes until dusk. When she was dead, her corpse was

---

[15] In this ritual context, black is a symbol of female substance. This association is drawn from the essential black color of "menstrual blood" *(mem khaim)*.

lowered to the ground, and male ritual elders began to cut her body. Her head, which was decorated with black pigment and the head-dress of a female ritual elder, was removed and lashed to one of the *bokhuur* pandanus trees to decay. Once again, the reviled gall bladder was removed and discarded. Finally, different male and female parts of her body were distributed by the male ritual elders to the ritual participants, while the remaining bodily parts were piled beneath the *bokhuur* pandanus tree that did not contain the severed head. This ritual enhancement of the fertility of the pandanus trees and, by implication, humans was reinforced once again through prescribed acts of ritual anthropophagy.

As in the case of the male victim in the first performance, the fat and flesh of her thighs and upper arms (female substance) were presented to those initiated men who were not ritual elders. In this ritual phase, the morsels were eaten in a raw (not steamed and roasted) state. The imagery is quite different in this context, for the cannibalistic act of consuming raw female parts of an enemy woman is not that of a warrior, but rather that of a male sorcerer. Indeed, the defilement of a major enemy warrior is not an issue in this context. However, an Oksapmin woman is held to be the most feared of all *tamam* witches, for she possesses the most powerful witchcraft bodily substances, *sacrae,* and rites. The reduction and destruction of her malevolent female substance, therefore, was the major emphasis of this second phase of the great pandanus rite. Thus, initiated men, who were dressed in the guise of male sorcerers and wielded sorcery implements, ate pieces of her thighs and upper arms, and all male participants were expected to participate in this act as "sorcerers." To protect themselves from the powerful pollution of these ingested morsels, these men also consumed bone marrow (male substance) from both wild boars (cooked) and the victim's body (raw). The cannibalistic consumption of bone marrow draws significance from analogous acts that are performed by the male lineage agnates of a woman during her funerary rites. In the great pandanus rite, however, men's consumption of both wild boar and human bone marrow (male substance) *and* human flesh and fat (female substance) is believed to have strengthened the fertility of both humans and pandanus trees through the ritual and (subsequently) procreative acts of the male participants. Ultimately, an abundance of fine crops of large, oily pandanus nuts and strong sons with glistening skins would demonstrate the efficacy of the rite.

Fragments of the victim's genitalia (female substance) were presented to both female ritual elders and ordinary initiated men to eat raw. As in the previous case of the male victim, these cannibalistic acts were performed in recognition of the Bimin-Kuskusmin ritual and social status that had been conferred upon the victim through sacrifice, suffering, and bodily decoration. For the female ritual elders, the symbolic significance of this act is linked to their special anthropophagic obligations in the mortuary rites of paramount female elders of their clans. In the great pandanus rite, the ritual strength that was wrought in the victim through sacrifice, suffering, and ritual decoration is believed to have been incorporated in the female ritual elders of all Bimin-Kuskusmin through their consumption of the victim's ritually purified uterus and vagina. These female ritual elders then strengthened the efficacy of this cannibalistic performance by eating cooked parts of the lower belly fat of cassowaries, which is another purified female substance in all ritual contexts. Above all, however, the great androgynous mystical power of Bimin-Kuskusmin female elders is believed to have prevailed over the malevolent witchcraft power of the female Oksapmin victim.

For the ordinary initiated men, the cultural significance of this same act is associated with their mortuary cannibalism of genital parts of a dead wife. In the great pandanus rite, however, the initiated men who ate the victim's genitalia are believed to have reduced the threat of her witchcraft capacity, which is concentrated in her genitals, and to have ensured the efficacy of the rite in promoting the fertility, propagation, and growth of both humans and pandanus trees. Severely contaminated by this form of ritual anthropophagy, these men also consumed cooked portions of wild boars' hearts, which are exceptionally powerful male substances in all ritual contexts. It was the female ritual elders, nevertheless, who not only purified the female victim's body, which they do for ordinary women in female initiation, but also destroyed her *tamam* witchcraft powers, which they do as the most deadly of witch-killers, through cannibalistic acts. They furthered the ritual transformation of the victim that the male participants had begun. In order to protect themselves from massive pollution through anthropophagic contact with the victim's genitalia, these female ritual elders also ate the genitalia of wild boars. Boar genitalia are considered to be ritually powerful and highly dangerous to all ordinary women, but their exceptional masculine power protects and strengthens the androgynous female ritual elders.

In this second phase of the great pandanus rite, the victim was both Oksapmin and female. Thus, the ritual anxiety about the relationship between polluted female substance and dangerous witchcraft capacity was even more pronounced than in the previous case of the male Oksapmin victim. Once again, both men and women were expected to eat all of the victim's lower belly fat, which is an especially polluting part of the "female anatomy." But certain aspects of the female victim's *"male* anatomy," especially those parts in close proximity to her genitalia or breasts, also had to be ritually removed or reduced in dangerous power. Indeed, some of the male substance of the female Oksapmin victim was considered to be very powerful, but in a very polluting and dangerous manner that was inimical to the efficacy of the rite. To offset the contaminating effects of both female and male substance in the victim's body, male participants became more prominent in this second phase of the rite, but women also performed a central anthropophagic act in order to weaken and destroy the victim's polluting female substance.

The women's ritual contribution is symbolically linked to the funerary obligations of a dead woman's female lineage agnates and cognatic kin to eat her lower belly fat. In the great pandanus rite, analogous acts are believed to have strengthened female ritual power and fertility with respect to both the "natural" reproduction of children and the ritual increase of pandanus harvests. The matter was complicated, however, by a great fear of the female victim's menstrual and witchcraft pollution, which are linked and concentrated in her lower belly fat. Thus, when initiated women ate this contaminated lower belly fat, they also consumed the strong male substance of the hearts, bone marrow, and genitalia of wild boars. Because the boar genitalia, as among the most ritually powerful of male substances, were also dangerous to them, they also ate the ritually strong, but sexually ambiguous lower belly fat of the androgynous cassowaries for ritually protective purposes. In the normal course of ordinary female mortuary rites, female agnatic and cognatic kin of a dead woman do not engage in these ritually protective measures, for the lower belly fat of normal women is not

especially polluting to other women. In contrast, the female Oksapmin victim's belly fat is that of a *tamam* witch.

The initiated men who participated in this aspect of the second
phase of the rite were explicitly linked to several distinct male images in ritual speeches. The first image was associated with the
peculiar ability of male *tamam* witches to neutralize the power of
both male and female substances through cannibalism. In the great
pandanus rite, some male participants were adorned in the grotesque
manner of male *tamam* witches and bore the malevolent implements of witchcraft rites. In the ritual guise of witches, they are
believed to have reduced the threat of the pollution of the victim's
female substance by eating her lower belly fat. Because they also
neutralized the highly valued fertility of the victim's ritually
transformed female substance, however, they were obliged to alter-
nate in consuming first pieces of her lower belly fat and then morsels
of the genitalia of wild boars. Indeed, the boar testicles and penises
that they ate are believed to have mystically renewed and in-
vigorated the reproductive powers of the victim's female substance.
These reproductive powers are also associated with male parts of
women. In the great pandanus rite, the victim's fertile substances
(male) had been damaged by the witchcraft powers of both the victim herself (by "natural" process) and the male "witch" performers
(by ritual process). To ensure that the victim's fertility was completely restored for ritual purposes, these male performers also
anointed her genitalia with boar semen, which is a ritually potent
male substance. In addition, their ritually prescribed "witchcraft"
practices had suppressed the dangers of the victim's menstrual and
witchcraft capacities, which are both aspects of female substance.
The ritually constructed and "naturally" weaker male form of
witchcraft was held to be a positive antidote to the dreaded substantial aspects of the female *tamam* witch in strengthening the efficacy
of the rite.

The second image was linked to the capacity of male sorcerers to
transform both male and female substances into strong male
substances by anthropophagic acts. In the great pandanus rite,
some men wore the ritual regalia of male sorcerers, which displays
both red (male) and black (female) feathers, and carried the
decorated bone daggers and other implements of sorcery. They ate
morsels of the female victim's lower belly fat (female substance) and
adjacent abdominal muscle (male substance). By means of this can-

nibalistic act, they destroyed much of her feared pollution and significantly strengthened her fertility. They also consumed small amounts of boar semen (male substance), however, in order to counteract the bodily contamination that they had acquired from her polluted female substance.

The third image drew upon the transformative power of the male trickster *gabruurian*. In the great pandanus rite, several male performers wore the bizarre regalia of *gabruurian,* which displayed both male and female ritual insignia. They are believed to have been central figures in the ritual transformation of the female victim from a menstruous, polluting *tamam* witch into a powerful, androgynous Bimin-Kuskusmin female ritual elder. This transformation was effected by their cannibalistic consumption of pieces of her abdominal muscle and pelvic bone marrow, which are both male substances that are bound up with a woman's menstrual and witchcraft capacities. In this manner, they participated in the ritual creation of a power and purity in the body and mystical identity of the female victim that denied her "naturally" threatening qualities. Like the acts of many other ritual performers, their participation permitted the bodily substance of the victim to become a powerful ritual artifact and an integral part of the substance of those ritual performers who sought to promote fertility in themselves and in their sacred pandanus trees through highly patterned forms of cannibalism. The ritual impersonators of *gabruurian,* however, were also profoundly polluted by their anthropophagy, and they remedied this contamination in part by eating the abdominal muscle and pelvic bone marrow (male substances) of both wild boars and cassowaries. Despite this purificatory act, their sacred androgynous and female characteristics were transformed into male features in the traditional manner of *gabruurian,* and they shed their bizarre regalia and adorned themselves with male headdresses and bodily decorations. When the ritual impersonators of *gabruurian* had reverted to male characters, the final anthropophagic act of the great pandanus rite was complete.

CONCLUSION

The cannibalistic aspects of the great pandanus rite illuminate a number of variations and constancies in Bimin-Kuskusmin cultural constructions of anthropophagy, which are bound to elaborate ideas about bodily substances and their significance. Delicate balances of male and female substances, which are represented in male and female victims, performers, sacrificial animals, and foods — and in their metaphoric and metonymic alignments — are articulated in complex ritual acts. Particular symbolic constructions achieve a certain ritual efficacy by overcoming substantial pollution through an anthropophagic adjustment in bodily balances. In turn, aspects of this rite are elucidated by more or less analogous cannibalistic practices and beliefs in other contexts and by a variety of culturally significant patterns of substances (see Poole 1976, 1977, 1981a, b, 1982).

The Bimin-Kuskusmin map of cultural differences in cannibalism provides a broad context for identifying both the sacrificial Oksapmin victims and the traditionally distinctive anthropophagic features of the rite. Fundamental considerations of gender, kinship, ritual status, and bodily substance link putative ritual practices of cannibalism within the great pandanus rite to myriad anthropophagic beliefs and practices that are portrayed in ethnohistory, myth, folktale, warfare, sexual relations, marriage, ritual relations, and mortuary or fertility rites. Different constellations of the cultural construction of cannibalism are woven from different ideas about fertility, reproduction, growth, bodily substances, foods, strength, power, ritual efficacy, and pollution, all of which are bound up with distinctions and transformations of gender. Images of initiated Bimin-Kuskusmin men and women, alien men and women, ritual elders, major enemies, sorcerers, tricksters, and witches, as well as cassowaries and wild boars, are implicated in these constructions. Complex notions about types and balances of "natural" substances in relation to categories or images of persons mark the appropriate patterns of Bimin-Kuskusmin cannibalism in a range of different contexts. But always, whether or not Bimin-Kuskusmin anthropophagy is portrayed in belief or in practice, all acts of eating human flesh are elaborate metaphoric, ritual, and symbolic constructions. Indeed, the great pandanus rite emphasizes the *cultural* construction of Bimin-Kuskusmin cannibalism.

It should be apparent, therefore, that a more comprehensive ethnography of Bimin-Kuskusmin anthropophagy must consider both "fact" and "fantasy" as cultural constructions. Indeed, for

Bimin-Kuskusmin the idea of cannibalism implicates a complex amalgam of practice and belief, history and myth, and matter-of-fact assertion or elaborate metaphor. The subject enters into crass sexual insults, ribald jokes, and revered sacred oratory. It is displayed in the plight of famine, the anguish of mourning, and the desperation of insanity. It marks aspects of the social life-cycle from the impulses of the unborn to the ravages of the ancestors. It is projected outward as a feature of the ethnic landscape and inward as an idiom of dreams, possession states, and other personal fantasy formations. In different contexts it may be seen as an inhuman, ghoulish nightmare or as a sacred, moral duty. But always it is encompassed by the order of ritual and the tenor of ambivalence. The Bimin-Kuskusmin have no single term for "cannibalism," for the ideas that are implicated are constructed for particular purposes of discourse that emphasize different dimensions of the phenomenon. In the great pandanus rite, however, as well as in its related contexts, one can discern some more or less common features that form and inform many Bimin-Kuskusmin cultural constructions of anthropophagy. This essay has been constituted as an ethnographic exploration of those features.

REFERENCES

ARENS, W.   1979.   *The Man-Eating Myth.* New York: Oxford University Press.
BARTH, FREDRIK.   1971.   Tribes and Intertribal Relations in the Fly Headwaters. *Oceania* 41(3):171-191.
————.   1975.   *Ritual and Knowledge among the Baktaman of New Guinea.* New Haven: Yale University Press.
BRUMBAUGH, ROBERT C.   1980.   *A Secret Cult in the West Sepik Highlands.* Ph.D. Dissertation, State University of New York at Stony Brook, University Microfilms, No. 80-17, 749, Stony Brook, New York.
DORNSTREICH, MARK D., and GEORGE E. B. MORREN.   1974.   Does New Guinea Cannibalism Have Nutritional Value? *Human Ecology* 2(1):1-12.
POOLE, FITZ JOHN PORTER.   1976.   *The Ais Am.* Ph.D. Dissertation, Cornell University, University Microfilms, No. 77-11, 008, Ithaca, New York.
————.   1977.   The Ethnosemantics of *Yemen:* Food Prohibitions, Food Transactions, and Taro as Cultigen, Food, and Symbol among the Bimin-Kuskusmin. Paper presented to the 76th Annual Meeting of the American Anthropological Association, Houston.
————.   1981a.   *Tamam:* Ideological and Sociological Configurations of "Witchcraft" among Bimin-Kuskusmin. *Social Analysis* 8:58-76.
————.   1981b.   Transforming "Natural" Woman: Female Ritual Leaders and

Gender Ideology among Bimin-Kuskusmin. *Sexual Meanings* (S. B. Ortner and H. Whitehead, eds.), pp. 116-165. New York: Cambridge University Press.

————. 1982. The Ritual Forging of Identity: Aspects of Person and Self in Bimin-Kuskusmin Male Initiation. *Rituals of Manhood* (G. H. Herdt, ed.), pp. 99-154. Berkeley: University of California Press.

RIVIERE, PETER G. 1980. Review of Arens' *The Man-Eating Myth. Man* 15 (1):203-205.

STEADMAN, LYLE B. 1975. Cannibal Witches among the Hewe. *Oceania* 46 (2):114-121.

Cannibalism Among Women in the Eastern Highlands of Papua New Guinea

GILLIAN GILLISON

Before it was abandoned in the early 1960s, cannibalism among the Gimi-speaking peoples of the Eastern Highlands of Papua New Guinea[1] was looked upon as a practice that women invented and in which they were especially prone to engage.[2] Adult males who ate

---

[1] Between October 1973 and September 1975, together with my husband David Gillison and our daughter Samantha, I carried out fieldwork in (as it then was) Lufa Sub-District, Eastern Highlands District, Papua New Guinea. In this endeavor I gratefully acknowledge the financial support of the National Science Foundation and the Canada Council.

[2] Despite the claim by some women that Gimi men also practiced cannibalism, and despite the sexually undifferentiated cannibalism reported for certain other Eastern Highlands societies (e.g., Berndt 1962), the evidence presented in this essay amply confirms that, in Gimi society, this activity was exclusively associated with women. In addition, the epidemiology of kuru, a neurological disease found among the Fore and their Gimi neighbors and transmitted during the eating or handling of infected human tissue, substantiates men's assertions that women and young children were the main practitioners. The pattern of kuru's disappearance after cannibalism was abandoned suggests that females often contracted the disease as adults but that the afflicted males were younger, indicating that males were exposed to kuru (which has a 20-year incubation period) as children who shared their mothers' meals (cf. Lindenbaum 1979:26).

GILLIAN GILLISON lives in New York City. Having received her doctorate from the City University of New York, she is now writing a book on Gimi myth and ritual theater.

The author wishes to express her appreciation to Marilyn Strathern for her insights and perceptive critical comments during the development of certain central ideas presented here. She also thanks the editors of this volume for their many helpful suggestions.

human flesh were referred to as "nothing men," as men of low status who, by eating the dead, made themselves weak like women. Eating human meat drained a man of his strength so that he was limply helpless before his enemies on the battlefield. The questions I pose with regard to the Gimi are: Why was cannibalism thought to fertilize women but to debilitate men? Why was it treated as an inevitable expression of woman's nature but as the hallmark of a contemptible femininity in men?

Gimi is a language spoken by about 10,000 people. Like most New Guinea Highlanders, Gimi cultivate sweet potatoes and keep pigs in a semidomesticated state. A Gimi village is typically made up of some 20 compounds spaced along a mountain shelf within an altitudinal range of 1,700 to 2,000 meters. Each compound houses about 10 to 25 adults, organized around a patrilineal core. Before the *Pax Australiana* of the early 1960s, smaller, more compact settlements were strategically perched on inaccessible ridge-tops and surrounded by wooden stockades. While women bore the main burden of subsistence (as they still do), men and initiated boys kept themselves in a state of combat readiness, sleeping together in one or two large oval men's houses that dominated the compound's muddy clearing. Then, as now, married women lived virilocally. A wife resided with her mother-in-law or co-wife, her young children, unmarried daughters, and several pigs, in a small round dwelling at the compound's edge. Men point out that this perimeter of women's houses once served as an early warning of the enemy's advance in predawn raids: an alarm from an outlying woman's house woke the men and gave them precious moments to rally.

The men's house, with its barrackslike rows of sleeping platforms, is still today strictly off limits to women, whose menstrual blood spoils the strength of warriors and damages the emerging manhood of young males. Women are forbidden to enter the men's house mainly because hidden there are sacred bamboo flutes which no female or uninitiated male should ever see. The flutes, called "birds" and said to represent penises, are secret repositories of immense supernatural powers to transform boys into men and to make gardens fertile, pig herds prosper, the rain forest productive, and rituals effective. Despite actions by missionaries in the early 1960s to expose the flutes to women and to destroy their mystical efficacy, the instruments still figure as the central objects in male initiation rites and men still extract a vow from every novice that he kill any woman who lays eyes upon them. The flutes are the raison d'etre for the residential segregation of the sexes, a fundamental principle of Gimi social organization which was deliberately violated during the practice of cannibalism. In the past, Gimi men say, women dismembered a man in his garden, carried the sections of his body inside the men's house and remained secluded there for days while they further divided up, ate, and digested his flesh. We may wonder if, during that time, the women saw the forbidden flutes which were (and are) kept wrapped in banana leaves and hidden in the rafters. That men would describe the act of women entering the men's house — let alone that they would allow it — reveals how important it was to men that women practice cannibalism.

When a man dies, men carry his body inside his mother's or wife's house and lay him on a mat of dried pandanus leaves. In the small dark hut, his female relatives crowd around him, swatting away flies, lifting and caressing his limbs, pressing their mouths onto his face and chest, beating their breasts, throwing themselves onto the hard packed-mud floor, and wailing for long periods of the day and night. After about four or five days, his male matrikin move him on a litter to his garden and bury him in a wooden chamber built inside a hillside vault. In the past, they installed him on a wooden platform built two to three meters off the ground amid a stand of sugarcane or bamboo (once a standard method of disposing of the dead in many parts of the Eastern Highlands). Supposedly, men left the body there slowly to decompose among the man's own produce, but the women, unable to contain their sorrow, secretly dragged him off the funeral bed and ate him. I discuss the fate of female corpses below.

The account men give of the first cannibal meal is like a myth in that it resembles the Gimi myth of origin, the myth of bamboo flutes (see below). But it also serves as a condensed account of what actually took place during the death ritual when a man was eaten. In one man's words:

A man was put in a tree to rot, that is what men (intended). But his sisters and his mothers objected, thinking: "He must not be allowed to rot! We will save him!" When the men went back to the compounds, the women tricked their husbands, each one saying: "Oh, I have to go to the garden now (to collect food for the evening meal)." . . . But secretly the women made a pact among themselves! . . . (and they gathered in the garden of the dead man) . . .

The women climbed onto the platform and took the body down to the ground, to the base of the bamboo, and cut it up. The women filled their net bags and walked back to the compound. Their husbands thought: "My wife went to get some food and is back." But the wives secretly said together: "We want to cut up this man. If even one man hears us, he will tell the others and they will beat us. So let us keep a secret!"

You see, men built a platform for the body and said: "We will not eat him." But the women tricked us! They rammed the meat into bamboo (cooking vessels) together with wild greens they had secretly collected and arrived at the men's house (while the men were away). They took the meat inside and . . . when their husbands returned, the men *saw* and exclaimed: "Ah! They are eating!" [cf. Berndt 1962:276]

At that moment, say the men, when they discovered what a "terrible thing" women had done, they closed the doors of the men's house, saying to the women inside:

"Who went and pulled this man down (off the platform) and cut him?"

And the women answered: "She and she and she pulled him down and we cut him."

"All right," said the men. "You (women) finish eating him. Later, when you are done, that woman and that one and that one, however many of you cut this man, for (all of you) we shall kill pigs." In that way the men took note of the women.

And the women who had pigs spoke up and said: "Yes, I will kill (my) pigs." And so, when the man was completely eaten, we held the death rites (by) killing pigs.

For as long as it took the women to eat and digest the man, they were secluded. The men outside kept track of the women's meal by sending into the men's house as observers several men of low status and several boys who also ate the human meat. These males and one or two of the women were instructed to watch who ate what part of the corpse so that they could later report this information to the brothers and sons of the deceased. Based upon this accounting, the men prepared to distribute to each woman cooked sections of pork[3]

---

[3] Some 30 years ago, before the increase in numbers of pigs, marsupials were the main source of ritual meat. (In densely forested regions and in small-scale distributions, marsupials are still used, suggesting that Gimi rituals once had fewer participants.) Although men hunt marsupials and women nurture pigs, I regard the "wild" (*kore*) and semidomesticated animals as symbolic equivalents: both represent edible beings with female attributes captured or owned by men and infused with spirit (*kore*). The possum, whose fur and marsupial pouch men liken to female pubic hair and the womb, is also used in men's chants to symbolize the secluded male initiate and in women's myths to stand for the child *in utero* (a creature generally regarded as male, i.e., as the product of penetration by the male). The possum symbolizes female reproductive organs that *conceal the male being*. Below, I suggest that, by "forcing" the women cannibals to eat such food (i.e., pigs = marsupials = human fetus = internalized male), men "drive out" or "cause to be born or excreted" its equivalent (i.e., the devoured man's "soul").

that corresponded exactly to the parts of the man's body she had reportedly consumed.

A Gimi man (aged about 35 years) describes this part of the death ritual:

When the women were finished eating we asked: "Have you women completely finished?" It was wrong if any part of the man remained (uneaten) when we started to kill pigs. It was wrong to eat a man and pigs at the same time.

The men killed about five to ten pigs. The brothers of the dead man, his sons, his younger brothers, his older brothers—these men killed their pigs and butchered them. A man died. The women ate him. We killed pigs to make (the feast for) the death rites.

We asked the women: "Who ate his head?" One woman, the one who watched what went on, answered: "That woman ate his head." And we men said: "All right, give her the head of a pig (to eat)."

And we handed it to her. . . . "His back, who ate his back?" The woman who watched spoke out: "Oh, *she* ate his back." Then we gave her the back of a pig. "His hand, who ate his hand?" And that same woman called out: "Oh, *that* one did!" And so we gave to that woman the hand of a pig. We gave the two hands, the right and the left. And those two women took (the right and the left) hands of pigs.

In this fashion, as Gimi report, all the parts of the man's body were named and the corresponding parts of pigs distributed in order: after the hands were the upper and lower legs and the chest (right and left sides), intestines, heart, lungs, liver, stomach, and other internal organs. Last were the genitals:

"His penis, who ate his penis?"[4] we men asked. "She did." And we gave that woman the penis of a pig. "His testicles, who ate his testicles?" "She did," said the one who watched. And so we cut the testicles off a pig and gave them to her. They were hers! And that was it. Finished!

As each woman was called outside the men's house by name and took into her hands sections of pork that matched the parts of the man she was said to have eaten, she ended her confinement.

Death rites performed during the period of fieldwork may be seen

---

[4] But according to a different male informant: "The penis was never eaten. It was buried at the base of a bamboo plant. And the vagina was never eaten. It was buried at the base of the bamboo, too, and of the pandanus. (The women) ate only the meat on the bones!" A third male informant remembered that, at about age six, he "wandered" into the men's house while the women were breaking open bamboo vessels that contained the cooked flesh of a Big Man. Noticing that the boy was small for his age, the women good-naturedly offered him the Big Man's penis to eat, saying that it would make him quickly grow big. The idea that, in Gimi cannibalism, "penis = whole body" is explored below.

as surviving fragments of this ritual. After four or five days of mourning, the dead man is buried in his garden. But the women still proceed to the deceased's men's house and remain there for days until his sons and brothers present them with sections of cooked pigs. The pigs are butchered in ceremonial style: internal organs are removed, cleaned, and set aside, and the carcass is completely boned, leaving the singed hide and subcutaneous fat in its entirety. This procedure (used whenever pork is ritually exchanged) creates four categories of meat: the whole skin; the bones with some meat adhering; the meat; and the innards. On occasions when I was present, the apportionment of these cuts of meat corresponded to accounts of what transpired when cannibalism was said still to be part of the death ritual. The pigs' flat, fat-saturated skins were cut into rectangular slabs and distributed to the ragged, clay-covered mourners who arrived from other villages. As one man remembers: "We gave out only the skins. Heads, limbs, ribs, backbones—all the bones of the pigs—and meat and innards could not go to outsiders! . . . The men who cut up the pigs gave these parts to the women who ate the man!"

The partially cooked pigs' limbs and innards nowadays handed out to women as they emerge from funerary seclusion were, I suggest, once offered to cannibals in exchange for the deceased's digested spirit. In this view, men's gift of pork precipitated women's departure from the men's house because it replaced their human meal and induced them to leave behind the residue, the bones.[5] About a year after this ritual transaction,[6] men carry the dead man's bones to cordyline trees planted at the borders of his garden and to mountain caves, hollow trees, and other sequestered places in the clan hunting grounds. The dark cavities in trees and rocks, men say, are like "vaginas"; the forks in branches, like "women's crotches."

---

[5] That is, the large bones. Small bones of forearm, wrist, hand, and foot were emulsified and used to make "blood pudding." "When the women finished eating the man—the skin and the meat were finished first—they ate the blood. They put the bones in the sun and gathered wild parsley and greens and put them on banana leaves underneath the bones. . . ." As the sun dried the bones, the fatty marrow dripped onto the absorbent bed of parsley. The women pounded the dried bones into powder and added it, together with the blood, to the saturated parsley. They wrapped these ingredients in the banana leaf and steamed them in a bamboo tube or earth oven.

[6] During the year after a man's death, his mother customarily wears his jaw, encased in netted possum fur, on a string around her neck. At the back of her head hangs his skull, concealed inside a small net bag.

When new growth appears on shriveled, dead-looking cordyline stakes, when marsupials emerge from nests in trees like babies "slipping out" amidst "woman's pubic hair," when rivers flow like "menstrual blood" or "semen," they are said to represent reissuances of human life. Because of their spontaneous appearance in the world, these "wild things" are symbols of the creativity of ancestral spirit.

The "uterine" crevices in the forest where men's bones are deposited and whence their spirits emerge transformed, symbolically, exist in male — not female — bodies. Marsupials' nesting holes, for example, are "vaginas" in the phallic torsos of trees. In men's initiation songs, a tree is likened to the whole body of a man as though it were a penis, the mouth or fontanel (lit: "top" + "mouth"), a urethra. Birds that feed upon fruits in a tree's upper branches and then, startled, fly away en masse, are compared to unborn children taking nourishment during gestation before being born in an explosive discharge. In this image, the tree's fruit-laden upper extremities and the birds that eat there are the culmination of a life-force rising through the tree's hollow trunk until it bursts forth, like an ejaculation, at the crown. The insertion of a man's bones in the tree's "lower mouth" (marsupial nest) initiates this upward thrust and results in the creation of an "upper mouth" at the "head." As a symbol of a man reborn into the forest afterworld, a tree is a gigantic self-transforming penis in which the reproductive powers and orifices of both sexes combine.

From this perspective, cannibalism was the first stage in a process to regenerate the dead, part of the means to maintain the continuity of existence by transferring human vitality to other living things. This transmigration was carried out through metaphoric sexual intercourse, in which a man's whole body functioned as a penis: by "going inside" women cannibals, his body was transformed into a dispersible set of spirit-laden bones; by "going inside" symbolic female orifices in the forest, his bones bore issue, that is, the spirit within them caused rivers to flow and animals and plants to appear spontaneously in the world. Gimi equate bones with the penis outside the context of ritual. Men state that when a man ejaculates, the stuff inside his skull travels down through his spine and into his penis, which becomes uncharacteristically hard and erect — like a bone. At the same time, the rest of his body, which is usually upright, and his bones, which are ordinarily hard, become prone and soft, respectively, because some amount of this vital fluid is uncontrollably expelled from the head. "When we have sex with [lit: "go up inside"] women, we die," one man allowed. "We are left with no strength [lit: "bone" + "thing"]. We are limp in every part [of our bodies]." These "little deaths" or "little devourings" represent irretrievable losses of the limited supply of vital male fluid and therefore cause a gradual reduction in stature—the literal using up (or "eating") of the body-matter—of Gimi men as they age.

Considering the close associations between a man's whole body, especially the hard parts, the bones, and his penis, I suggest that women's theft and consumption of the male corpse were ritual attempts to acquire a penis, that women occupied the men's house for as long as they possessed their ill-gotten male thing and that they departed the moment men's offer of a replacement symbolically compelled them to give it up. Furthermore, I suggest that during the confinement, during the dead man's passage through the cannibals' bodies, his body was feminized, that is, it was endowed with a "vagina" or "mouth." This feminization transformed the devoured, lifeless man into a mobile spirit-being—a "body" in the form of an erect, hollow penis with female orifices (as are bones, trees, birds[7] and, archetypically, flutes). Once released from inside the female, this male soul had the capacity parthenogenetically to bring forth every kind of life, to "feed" and regenerate the Gimi wilderness. In these terms, men's gifts of pork prevented a universal power from becoming permanently ensconced in women cannibals, a power that enabled women to exclude men from the men's house and from the clan forest, places whose sacred confines bestow male identity.

Before I examine the myth of the flutes as a means to substantiate these interpretations of Gimi cannibalism and before I address questions posed at the outset regarding the effects of human flesh upon the vitality of male and female consumers, let me clarify less abstract features of the relations between the sexes that are implied in my description of the cannibal ritual. When I speak of the cannibals as female and of the ones devoured as in-group male, I make this generalization both in the literal sense that women and children

---

[7] Birds' anatomy lends itself to this image of "body = phallus with female opening." Most male birds have no external copulatory organ like the penis but ejaculate from a hole on the underside, the cloaca, which is identically situated on the body of the female. During copulation, sperm is transferred from male to female by direct contact between the two cloacas.

were the main practitioners and in the symbolic sense that the eating of female corpses, a regular occurrence, did not count. When a woman was eaten, men rarely presented the cannibals with pigs ritually to retrieve her bones, nor did they disperse them in garden or forest. In effect, the one devoured was barred from an afterlife.[8]

Sagan suggests that when some members of a society are cannibals and others are not, "the society is ambivalent in its attitude" (Sagan 1974:12) and there develops a "split" in institutional norms:

> If there exists both the desire to abandon cannibal behavior and the desire to continue it, one resolution of this conflict is to assign certain members of the culture to engage in cannibal behavior while the others look on from a safe distance.

According to Gimi men, women dismembered, cooked, and consumed the dead surreptitiously and without ritual.

> All the women of the village gathered. The man's sisters were so sorry for him they could not let him rot. His own mother ate him but she did not cut him. . . . His mother's co-wife or his father's brother's wife did most of the cutting. . . .
> All our mothers tell us: "A man was the sweetest thing on earth to eat!" They cooked the fleshy parts in bamboo (containers) and the limbs in an earth oven. . . . Men cut pigs. (As for human meat) we just looked. But women cut men. They would grab a piece raw and quickly ram it into bamboo. . . .

In coarse playlets which they still perform during celebrations at marriages and initiations, women themselves portray their meal as an orgy. In the first scene of one performance, a warrior-dummy made from net bags, shot full of arrows and "near death," is carried on the shoulders of a lone comrade through enemy lines toward home. Several of the "enemy" violently take hold of him and shout encomiums to their clan's rivers and to their ancestors whose spirits congregate inside caves at the rivers' hidden sources. The men's loud

---

[8] I have no data on the frequency of cannibalism. Certainly, it was not always practiced but was especially likely to occur if the deceased was a man of importance. Women say that any Gimi might eat the dead but that some men preferred not to indulge. Male informants, on the other hand, are adamant: cannibalism was practiced only by females, uninitiated boys, and men of lowest caliber, including sorcerers. Men say that firstborn males, females and enemies should not have been eaten. But women still act out eating the enemy and say they placed no restrictions upon in-group males. When a woman died (women say) her sisters, the daughters of her father and his brothers, did not eat her nor did her husband's own mother. Other women related to her husband, his sisters and his father's sisters, were allowed to consume her body, as was her own mother. But, in women's words, most cannibals were "nothing women," women with no important tie to the deceased. Cannibalism was, in this sense, a deliberately collective female activity.

praises are efforts to induce the life-force escaping from the "dying man" to fly to these mountain places there to increase the accumulation of male spirit belonging to the killers' clan. Suddenly, "wives" and "mothers" of the victorious men enter the hut, dance uproariously through the crowd and "force" the male players who surround the dummy to back away. At once shouting for joy and wailing and beating their breasts in sorrow, the women begin to "dismember" the "corpse": they pick it up, wrench it back and forth among them, and drop it torn and misshapen to the floor. Removing bamboo knives from their waistbands, the women "cut" the body, flinging "innards" (dried wild banana leaves) into the air as they fight greedily over choice parts. "I'll eat the penis. The head is mine! I put them aside for me!" shouts one woman. "I put aside that leg!" shouts another. "Give me! Give me! Give me!" the women all cry, as the audience laughs in appreciation of their poignant self-caricature.[9]

But outside the context of ritual enactment, women base their cannibal activities upon altruism and a determination to help men achieve eternal life.[10] Older women remember that human flesh had

---

[9] Berndt says that among certain neighbors of the Gimi "enemies are eaten just as readily as kin or affines" (Berndt 1962:270). While this may have been true of Gimi practice, it contradicts the statements of Gimi men who say that their enemies were outsiders utterly unworthy to be eaten and that they threw their despicable corpses into rivers whence their own kin might retrieve them. But given Gimi conventions of exogamy and virilocal residence, certain enemies of the village were related to some male residents as brothers-in-law and to their wives as brothers. This is the constellation of relations among the performers in this farce. The women who simultaneously wept and rejoiced were classificatory sisters of the "deceased" and wives of his "killers." For such women, the distinction between endo- and exo-cannibalism may not have been meaningful.

[10] Women's reasons for renouncing cannibalism under the edict of the Australian Administration were similar to their reasons for having practiced it. As one woman explained:

You see, when a man dies that is not the end (of him). He exists. If we do not eat him, he will return (to us as a White man).

In the past, we did not understand (this) and so we ate the dead. The White man came and explained these things to us . . . (that) our dead go to stay in Australia and come back (here) later as White men. (Knowing this), we do not cut up the dead anymore.

Certain ideas contained in this statement have their basis in an incident which occurred just before the area was pacified. According to Gimi accounts, an Australian Patrol arrived in the midst of a war in order to stop it. At the same time, Officers railed against eating the dead and against shooting *Paradisaea raggiana salvadorii*, a species of Bird of Paradise then disappearing from more densely populated areas of the Highlands because of increased hunting and deforestation which took place when the *Pax Australiana* freed men from the consuming preoccupation of war and allowed the inhabitants of fortified, ridge-top settlements greatly to extend the area of habitable and cultivable land. But to Gimi, the jointly issued prohibitions

a uniquely delectable sweetness (cf. Berndt 1962:271) but assert that their main desire was to prevent the ravages of decomposition. When the body of a man slain in battle was carried into his compound, the women surrounded it singing: "Come to me so you shall not rot on the ground. Let your body dissolve inside me!" Death begins the moment the last breath is silently exhaled through the fontanel and continues, hours or days later, as more vital "wind" (expanding intestinal gas) pushes its way out the anus. When this animating spirit-vapor finally departs, the body starts to follow and to disappear into the surroundings. But until disintegration is complete, the rotting flesh retains vestiges of the deceased's awareness. "We would not have left a man to rot!" women say. "We took pity on him and pushed him into our bamboo (cooking vessels) and ate him!" In several women's myths, the heroine is an old woman, a voracious cannibal who quietly saves the vital organs (lungs and livers) of the men she eats. Later she hands these organs over to a man who, by cooking them inside bamboo tubes, brings the devoured men back to life.

It seems to me that the conflict between the sexes over the eating of the dead described by men and the haste and disorder in which women supposedly conducted the actual cannibal meal were de rigueur: that is, they were *parts* of the death ritual, not preliminary to it, as men assert. The display of hostility overlays a tacit agreement that women would eat the corpse and that men would participate vicariously by watching. Although, in what I term the latter phase of the death ritual (and in what Gimi speak of as the ritual itself), the sexes stand opposed in the sense that men's presentation of pork to the secluded women was intended retroactively to "cancel" the disorder of their meal and so deprive women of the power lodged in them on account of having consumed male flesh,

---

against killing and eating men and birds were together construed as hindering white men, who were believed to incorporate the spirits of dead relations, from returning to the territory of their Gimi kinsmen. In Gimi belief, when a man dies, elements of his spirit eventually come to lodge with Birds of Paradise, especially with *P. raggiana*. When Gimi ate the spirit-laden flesh of men or birds, they retained the spirit inside Gimi territory so that it could not travel to Australia, a place Gimi now regard as the true afterlife. By restricting the movement of ancestral spirit, Gimi say, they unwittingly "closed the road" along which white men travel and prevented them from returning to their Gimi birthplace.

The apparent ease with which Gimi gave up cannibalism may be accounted for less by this rationalization than by an ever present and deeply felt ambivalence toward the practice.

men waited to carry out this deprivation until after they had used — or allowed women to use — their bodies (i.e., the female digestive/reproductive process) to catapult the dead man's spirit into the ancestral world. Although men state that a man should be left to rot and imply (in ritual farces) that mere exhortations can send his spirit to dwell at the headwaters, their ritual acts suggest that this ascent depends upon the male "passing through" women's bodies. Such an unacknowledged confluence of interest between the sexes would explain how women got hold of male corpses. As warriors men had access to the bodies of comrades and foes. If cannibalism was simply abhorrent, as men regularly say, they would likely have found ways to prevent it. It seems rather that Gimi cannibalism was an expression both of conflict between men and women and of their unspoken cooperation in the enactment of conflict, so that men could at one time speak of it as the outcome of women's utter unruliness yet treat it in ritual as a necessary part of a sublime passage to the afterworld.

In this light, women's cannibal activities enacted the first part of a mythic scenario, which equates the unbridled expression of women's desires with consumption of men's bodies and usurpation of male power. The sequence of ritual events by which women symbolically achieve their subversive ends — the theft of the corpse from its garden platform, the noiseless dismemberment of the body at the base of the platform, the hurried stuffing of the meat into bamboo cooking vessels — calls to mind the story of another epoch-making theft, one in which men wrest power — in the form of sacred bamboo flutes — from dominant women. The flutes (called "birds" and described as "penises") are paired, side-blown bamboo aerophones which men cut and test in the forest out of women's sight. They are made in the same two sizes and from the same wide varieties of wild bamboo as are the containers traditionally used to cook human flesh and innards. According to a myth which men say they keep secret from women:

A man heard strange sounds coming from his sister's "flute house" (the Gimi word for "menstrual hut").[11] He hid nearby in the tall grass and,

---

[11] As a menstruating or parturient woman, a woman with blood in her vagina (lit: "mouth") is secluded in a "flute house" (menstrual hut), so were cannibals, also women with "blood in their mouths" confined in a "flute house," i.e., in a house where flutes are kept, the "men's house."

when she went to her garden, he crept inside the hut and stole the flute that was ly-
ing at the head of her bed. When he put the instrument to his lips to play, he grew a
beard for the first time. He had not noticed that the flute's blowing hole was closed,
plugged up with his sister's pubic hair which, when he touched it, began to grow
around his mouth. He removed the hairy plug and began to make sounds.

When his sister returned from the garden, he told her: "You must give me the
thing that cries. You are not a man, but a woman. You can give it to me." She did
and forgot everything that happened and died. "So, today," men say, "whenever we
play (the flutes inside the men's house) women think: "I wonder what this is — some
strange bird perhaps — hiding inside the men's house and crying?" . . . But, to tell
the truth, it was once something that belonged *only* to women. It was not ours! We
men stole it!"[12]

In the flute myth, a man takes a flute (a "penis") from the bed or
body of his sister and makes her bleed for the first time. (In another
version of this myth, she keeps the instrument hidden under her
bark-string skirts and does not menstruate until her brother steals
it.) In cannibalism, women — sisters — take the dead man, whose
whole body (as I have suggested) stands for a penis, from the "body
of men" who had left him to rot on a funeral bed in his garden, and
make him bleed. Women got possession of the corpse through
trickery: they told their husbands they were going to gather
vegetables from their separate gardens but instead congregated in
the garden of the dead man to collect food of a different kind. The
cannibals feared that if even one man heard the incriminating
sounds of their cutting, all men would organize to disrupt women's
conspiracy and to take back the missing member of their sex. In the
flute myth, the mysterious sounds are ones which women are supposedly unable to identify and the secret society they symbolize is of
men. Men fear that if even one woman sees the flutes, all women will
understand what men have taken *from them* and, united (as a
"society"), will reclaim it.

Together, the narratives suggest that the female is the original
source of the flute/crying child/male body and that her greatest
desire is to get back her creation, again to enjoy the limitless powers
vested in it, powers secretly to organize the members of one's own sex
and so to create — which is, to dominate — Gimi society. In these
terms, cannibalism is tantamount to women's "repossession of the

---

[12] Nearly identical versions of the flute myth and of the associated male cult, known as the
nama cult (Read 1952, 1965), are found among virtually all Eastern Highlands language
groups, including the Gahuku-Gama (ibid.). See also Salisbury 1965; Newman 1965;
Langness 1974; Berndt 1962.

flute" and the flute is equivalent both to the corpse and to its bones—rigid, spirit-filled vessels which Gimi explicitly liken to the penis. The ritual recapitulation of the cannibal meal—the part-by-part presentation of pigs to women—may then be looked upon as men's counter-theft: by compelling the cannibals to relinquish the digested essence or pure spirit—the bones—of the man they ate, his male paternal relations may be seen, in effect, to have stolen back the flutes from women.

These symbolic transfers and counter-transfers of flutes between the sexes cannot be compared to exchanges in any simple sense, to cyclic alternations of gain and loss. Rather they signify the unceasing life-processes of mutual annihilation and rebirth. When women ate the male corpse/"recaptured the flute" they incorporated male spirit, sealing it inside their bodies so that it could not escape. When women owned flutes, their vaginas were sealed shut, plugged with pubic hair. They did not menstruate until vaginal openings were made by the brother's removing the pubic hair and stealing the flute. The bodies of flute-owning women were like the hollow trunks of trees inside which birds were trapped, flightless and silent,[13] like wombs filled with quiet (unborn) children, like unopened bamboo cooking vessels packed with male flesh and spirit. In this condition, the female cannibal was a completed or bisexual creature secluded in the men's house like a pregnant woman in confinement. Her "impregnation" was self-induced, a secret act of oral *self*-insemination (the eating of the "stolen" body/penis). Because they were unaware of what women did together noiselessly in the garden, living men could have no active role in reproduction. In this sense when female conspirators ate the corpse/when women owned flutes, all men were dead or "disappeared"; they were all associated with the silent contents of women's closed bodies.

By presenting the cannibals with a second course of pork, thus causing them to "excrete" the spirit-residue of the human first

---

[13] At the climax of a creation myth told by women to young children in the women's houses, a bride places the corpse of her baby brother inside a hollowed-out hoop pine and covers the opening at the top. Her husband tells her that gorgeous sounds will emerge from inside the sealed trunk but that she must not strike it. She disobeys him, sending birds of every species out the tree's "head" and into the world for the first time. In this and other tales, women convey the idea that *they*—in opposition to men (husbands)—are the heroic agents of men's (brothers') liberation.

course of their meal, I suggest, men metaphorically created openings in women thereby to release and bring to life the contents of their bodies. I derive this interpretation of the cannibal ritual from a comparison between it and the flute myth. After the mythic brother stole (i.e., detached) his sister's flute, he removed the hairy plug and put the instrument to his lips, simultaneously creating two "vaginas," one (low down) in her and another (high up) in himself. When he placed his newly bearded mouth to the flute's new blowing hole (around which men etch designs to represent "female pubic hair") he filled the instrument with his "wind" and pushed his euphonic spirit into the atmosphere. In this sense, flute playing is an act of self-creation by a man who stole a female orifice. It is analogous to the ritual feeding of cannibal women in this way: by "putting food in women's mouths" (food that was a replacement for the body of the dead man) living men "pushed out" the dead man's spirit. The spirit was identified not only with the deceased but also with the men themselves. It symbolized the self-made, fully realized male being recreated partly in the image of the female from whom he was liberated. The "born-again" male had a "vagina" (a bearded mouth).[14] He was complete unto himself and could dispense entirely with women.

Analyzed in this way, the flute myth and its ritual analogue, the seclusion of women cannibals inside the men's house and the laborious repetition of their meal, are expressions of Gimi men's desires to participate in or to induce their own births—their own *re*appearance in the world—by stealing from women the power to give birth. By feeding the cannibals spirit-laden (or "wild") animal meat, men enlivened the dead human flesh so that it "flew out" of woman, leaving her opened, emptied and mutilated by the male's violent leave-taking, like an eggshell broken by the fledgling's emergence, or like a charred and fractured bamboo cooking vessel that was once intact and full of food. At birth, the female is ruined and deserted because, during his passage through her body—from

---

[14] The anus is another such hairy, sound-producing, creative "female" orifice or "mouth" through which men's "wind" escapes into the atmosphere. During male initiation rites, the flute's blowing hole is explicitly compared to the anus and the music to the expulsion of intestinal gas. "Males create by a blowing movement (breath, wind) or by sound" (Dundes, citing Ernest Jones, 1976:225).

48   GILLIAN GILLISON

upper mouth to lower mouth, or vice versa—the male being (as penis, whole body, food, spirit, or bird) took *her* orifices, that is, *her* powers of reproduction. He emerges with/as the flute, a "penis" (rigid bamboo tube) with "womb" (hollow core) and "vagina" (blowing hole), stolen in transit, so to speak. And she is left fluteless and "unalive," in the primordial condition of the male.

CONCLUSION

Why did Gimi regard the consumption of human flesh as fertilizing to women but debilitating to men, leaving men, in the Gimi expression, "without bones"? To answer this question, posed at the outset, I have analyzed certain ritual practices associated with Gimi cannibalism in the light of the flute myth, the central myth of origin among the Gimi and other Eastern Highlands language groups.

According to my interpretation, the cannibal act itself, which Gimi men say was accomplished entirely without ritual (cf. Lindenbaum 1979:22; Berndt 1962:271) and against men's will, actually represented a preliminary stage of the death rite, in which women, acting in tacit cooperation with men, ate a male corpse in a deliberately chaotic, orgiastic manner. I compare this initial segment of the ritual with women's mythic possession of flutes, suggesting that the sacred instruments—symbolic penises—are equivalent to the "whole bodies" of devoured men. From this perspective, the recapitulation of the cannibal meal is the culminating part of the ritual, a substitution of pigs for the body of the devoured man, which I compare with men's mythic theft of flutes from women. This later segment, a re-doing—which is the undoing—of women's cannibalism, is equated with the primal imposition of social order by men in defiance of unruly women.

I suggest that in its *ritual* context women's "illicit" cannibalism brought about a merging of the sexes and a confusion of their roles which left women dominant: men presented food to women, reversing the daily pattern. Women's supposedly wilful consumption of a male corpse symbolically destroyed sexual distinctions in such a way as to threaten Gimi social and cosmic order. Men's careful matching of women to the parts of the male body each was reported carelessly to have eaten, brought about a retroactive organization of the cannibal deed tantamount to an enforced *separation of the sexes:* the gifts of pork, being identical to the parts of the male body, each symbolically replaced a specified limb or organ of the devoured man, so releasing him from a state of disintegration inside the female (comparable to the incomplete state of the fetus *in utero*). This ritually engineered separation—a "parturition"—occurred in such a way that the male being emerged from the female endowed with her powers (combining male and female in himself) and left her with nothing.

The symbolic absoluteness of women's loss and the reason their natures are said to be formed by "insatiable hunger" are connected, in my view, to the fact that Gimi treat reproductive power as if it were a *readily transmissible but indivisible thing (like a flute),* a concrete entity in the shape of a male body endowed with the reproductive organs of both sexes. This "thing" *cannot be shared* but, in the context of myth and ritual, is wholly possessed by one sex or by the other at different times. In other words, either the female is parthenogenetic or the male is. The former condition destroys world order; the latter, creates it.

If we think of fertility in this concrete and totalistic way and regard the current owners as male and the losers as female, then we may say that, in Gimi terms, the possession of reproductive power is synonymous with masculine identity and that this identity is extremely unstable, like a possession one is ever likely to lose or to acquire because it has a life of its own. The flute can never be certainly and finally owned because of its volatile nature, its eternal tendency to "fly away like a bird." In this sense, cannibalism is one means through which sexual identity can be symbolically altered. When women ate a man, they slept inside the men's house, suggesting that, for the duration of this ritual interlude, they had taken on male identity. It was as though women possessed the flutes in whose presence they resided and thereby deprived men, most of whom were now outside the men's house, of their male identity. In other words, while women had the flutes, men had none.

The implication of my analysis is that, from the perspective of *both* sexes, to be fertile—even, to be "alive"—is to possess the penis/male body/bones/flutes and to be weak—even, to be "dying"—is to lose this empowering object. It seems to follow, then, that men who were secluded inside the men's house with the women cannibals would, together with the women, ritually possess the flutes and become masculinized. But, in fact, the opposite held true: male cannibals were thought to have acted "like women" and on that account to be enfeebled, castrated, unfit for battle. Information that seems to contradict my conclusion actually strengthens it by highlighting the discrepancy between everyday life and ritual. In the former reality, men have penises, own flutes, and occupy the men's house; in the latter "reality," women do. I have argued that both sexes regard the initial phase of cannibal ritual as an enactment of women's desires, that is, as the dramatization of a fantasy that everyday reality is reversible and that sexual identity is alterable. In these terms, men who were secluded with the women enacted a *female* wish to usurp male power and therefore became "like women" in relation to the men outside: they became as powerless as those who are ordinarily bereft of flutes and can do no more than act out in ritual a desire to possess them. The desire I attribute to Gimi women may be compared to one Freud attributed to women in general when he said, "This wish for a penis is *par excellence* a feminine one" (1974:87).

REFERENCES

BERNDT, R. M. 1962. *Excess and Restraint: Social Control Among a New Guinea Mountain People.* Chicago: The University of Chicago Press.

DUNDES, ALAN. 1976. A Psychoanalytic Study of the Bullroarer. *Man* (n.s.) 2:220-238.

FREUD, SIGMUND. 1974(1933). Femininity. *Women and Analysis. Dialogues on Psychoanalytic Views of Femininity* (Jean Strouse, ed.), pp. 73-94. New York: Grossman.

GILLISON, GILLIAN. 1980. Images of Nature in Gimi Thought. *Nature, Culture and Gender* (Carol MacCormack and Marilyn Strathern, eds.), pp. 143-173. Cambridge, Eng.: Cambridge University Press.

LANGNESS, L. L. 1974. Ritual, Power and Male Dominance in the New Guinea Highlands. *Ethos* 2:189-212.

LINDENBAUM, SHIRLEY. 1979. *Kuru Sorcery.* Palo Alto: Mayfield.

NEWMAN, PHILIP L. 1965. *Knowing the Gururumba.* New York: Holt, Rinehart & Winston.

READ, KENNETH E. 1952. Nama Cult of the Central Highlands, New Guinea. *Oceania* 23:1-25.

————. 1965. *The High Valley.* New York: Scribner's.

SAGAN, ELI. 1974. *Cannibalism: Human Aggression and Cultural Form.* New York: Harper & Row.

SALISBURY, RICHARD F. 1965. The Siane of the Eastern Highlands. *Gods, Ghosts and Men in Melanesia* (P. Lawrence and M. J. Meggitt, eds.), pp. 50-77. Melbourne, Australia: Oxford University Press.

Human Leopards and Crocodiles

Political Meanings of Categorical Anomalies

CAROL P. MacCORMACK

INTRODUCTION

This analysis of discourse about cannibalism among the Sherbro of Sierra Leone is based on archival sources in Moyamba, Freetown, London, and church archives in Dayton, Ohio. It is also based upon ten years of intermittent fieldwork in the Sherbro country, including people's retrospective historical accounts, often given in a genealogical idiom. I have not purposefully done fieldwork on cannibalism, but in the context of events people do comment upon motives and behavior. Also, when one knows people well, they talk about things that lie below the surface of mundane conversation. I have never seen anyone eat human flesh, but Sherbros themselves do talk about it in the literal sense and in a figurative sense. It is the latter which is of particular interest, highlighting that which is socially constructive by reference to thoughts and deeds that promote the commonwealth in contrast with thoughts and deeds that are destructive and selfish.

Accusations of cannibalism are clearly a political weapon. The descendents of certain chiefly groups have told me how their

CAROL P. MacCORMACK is Senior Lecturer in Social Sciences at the London School of Hygiene and Tropical Medicine, University of London.

"fathers and mothers," their ancestors, went, in the early days of the Protectorate, to the District Commissioner with accusations that rival groups were "cannibals" and "not fit to rule." All this was duly minuted by diligent colonial officers. It is now in archives, and not to be taken as accurate "evidence" of actual flesh eating at all (see for example S.L.G.A. [Sierra Leone Government Archives], Native Affairs Department Letterbook, December 27, 1983). Therefore, it is a grave scholarly error for literal-minded historians to use this material without any anthropological interpretation (see, for example, Kalous 1974).

ENVIRONMENT AND HISTORY

The Sherbro coast of Sierra Leone is low-lying, parts of it awash in broad tidal rivers, swamps, and 180-inch wet-season rainfall. Road transport is sparse and difficult in this terrain, but coastal traders established "factories" (trade depots) for primary commodities, including slaves, from the 16th century onward (Rodney 1970:71). The Sherbro, deeply autochthonous people without a tradition of migration, were buffeted by wars for control of trade spheres. Migrants, especially the Mane, who in the 16th century came as overlords, and later the Mende who came to take advantage of trading opportunities, upset indigenous political organization. Some Sherbros adapted by making marriages with European traders, learning English, becoming trade brokers and being recognized as treaty chiefs when British colonial rule commenced in the late 19th century (Fyfe 1962). Sierra Leone is now, of course, a fully independent republic, but as late as 1977, dissatisfaction with the government caused disorder throughout the country. In parts of the Sherbro coast, houses were looted and burned, including the compound of a paramount chief, and lorry loads of political youth rampaged. The Human Leopard Society and the Alligator Society once again presented their profile.

SODALITIES

Sodalities, probably as deeply autochthonous as the Sherbro themselves, prepare children for the responsibilities of adulthood. They also maintain peace, public order, and public hygiene. They function as the sacred counterbalance to secular power of chiefs and present-day government officials. Poro for men (Little 1965, 1966), Sande for women (MacCormack 1979), Thoma initiating both genders (MacCormack 1980), and other sodalities protect the commonwealth. By contrast, the Human Leopard Society and the Human Alligator Society are the instruments of selfish power seekers in antisocial groups. However, having clearly drawn the lines between good and evil, I must emphasize that the Sherbro people have a high tolerance for ambiguity, and things are both what they seem and what they are not. When I tested this model of good and evil on Sherbro people, they readily acquiesced to the ideal, then the more candid or cynical would suck their teeth in a gesture of disgust and mutter: "but how do you think those Poro elders got their power?" (MacCormack [Notebook] 1976:521).

Leopards and crocodiles are common in the natural environment; at least 11 of the latter were shot in the Kagboro River while I was there in 1970. *Sonyay* is the Sherbro word for carnivorous crocodile, but the English translation of alligator was used in Colonial Office dispatches and has come into common parlance, so I shall refer to the Alligator Society even though we should think of the crocodile. Leopard and Alligator societies, although antisocial, are sodalities organized similarly to Poro, Sande, and Thoma. They all initiate members, function as a lifelong group, have "medicine" which is a tangible object linking humans to nonmundane sources of power, and initiates swear an oath of secrecy upon "medicine." Leopards and Alligators do this after allegedly eating cooked human flesh; Poro, Sande, and Thoma feast on animal and vegetable food. In the antisocial Leopard and Alligator sodalities, human fat is rubbed upon the "medicine" to energize or revive it, and sometimes rubbed upon the body to enhance one's personal charisma and power. Thus, the power derived from the rite is not limited to those who are assembled, but can be transported as "medicine" to others who are absent members, especially to strong political figures who allegedly pay considerable wealth for the "medicine" (S.L.G.A., Court Record Book, Moyamba District, May 1901–September 1903; February–November 1904; September 1908–May 1909; MacCormack [Notebooks] 1970:62–63, 1976:518–522). In a historical example, a newly appointed chief was alleged to have said to his Leopard Society fellows: "I have been selected for a Chief. I want all people to obey my word, so therefore you must go and catch a person for me" (S.L.G.A., Court Record Book, Moyamba District, September 1908–May 1909; see also February–November 1904). Political power of chiefs is largely an achieved status within an ideology of ascribed genealogical legitimacy (MacCormack 1972, 1974). Similarly, today government officials may rise to power swiftly and fall just as rapidly.

In a contemporary example, villagers talked guardedly of the absent town chief who allegedly received oil, rendered from a human, to pass on to his brother, a prominent national politician. The town chief "owed" two people in repayment. He reneged and disappeared to an unknown place with all the members of his large household. Because of the principle of corporate responsibility, the debt extended to all his kin in the cognatic descent system and, indeed, to all in the chiefdom who might be shielding him. A few local people had been menaced as they walked alone on deserted paths or roads (MacCormack [Notebook] 1976:518–522).

Both men and women are members of the Leopard and Alligator soicieities (S.L.G.A., Native Affairs Minute Paper 818 [1890]; General Minute Paper 2768 [1901]). Either gender may be wanted as a victim (S.L.G.A., Colonial Secretary's Office Judicial Proceedings, May 1931). Leopards go out as a group, but usually only one, covered with the skin of a leopard concealing face, head, and torso, leaps into view. Three or five small blades are set in a hand instrument and the jugular vein is often cut when the victim is caught (S.L.G.A., Court Record Book, Moyamba District, February–November 1904; MacCormack [Notebook] 1976:519). Today one may see this drama acted in dancing. In the evening simple neighborhood groups may gather to dance as light entertainment, or the dancing may have a rather dark message. In the latter case a dancer in the role of an unsuspecting person may be stalked in dance by the leopard figure (without costume).

Sherbros are farmers and fishermen; all go into the rivers and sea in dugout canoes but few can swim. The Alligator members are said to go under water in a self-propelled submarine canoe with the appearance of a crocodile. It overturns a fisherman's or trader's canoe and catches the victim, drawing him or her down into the water (S.L.G.A., District Commissioner's Shaingay Letterbook, 1906–1909; Law Court Archives, "The True Verdict or Cannibalism in the Hinterland of Sierra Leone," MS by D. F. Wilberforce, 1906–1913; MacCormack [Notebook] 1970:62–63).

An often repeated story of a cannibalism incident, told to me by a young man at the time people were being frightened by alleged Human Leopards, illustrates the ambivalence with which cannibals are regarded in a *social* dimension of analysis. In this account, told as history, a man accepted human oil or flesh, and was then required to repay the debt. He sent his son out alone to fish, but armed him with a cutlass and a spear, instructing him to use them if he was in danger. While the young man was fishing, the carved "crocodile" head of the cannibals' closed canoe surfaced. He jammed his spear inside the crocodile's mouth, killing one person inside. As the others attempted to climb out, he killed all the others with his cutlass. Thus the father freed himself from a flesh debt through his son (MacCormack [Notebook] 1976:520). By the same stroke he rid the area of a group of antisocial people. The teller praised the youth for destroying this group of dangerous and selfish people. However, the youth's own father had accepted human flesh and was one of that very group of antisocial people. He could certainly never say aloud that it is "good" to kill one's own powerful father (or mother), although young adults, restive under the authority of their parents, may sometimes harbor such emotions.

Females also talk of cannibalism. For example, Sherbro people do not eat monkey meat, although they say their ethnic neighbors to the south do eat it. One day, while I walked with two women, we talked of the damage monkeys do to ripening crops. The conversation broadened to include catching and eating monkeys. They said that pregnant women (who are always hungry) cannot resist the delicious smell and taste of monkey meat. They are especially susceptible to the temptation to eat human flesh, which tastes like monkey, when they are pregnant. Therefore they *never* cook or eat monkey. Once a pregnant woman has eaten human flesh, she must repay it. She will give birth to a child whom she must give to the cannibal society to settle the debt (MacCormack [Notebook] 1976:522).

When one eats human flesh in a cannibal society group, one becomes a debtor and must give someone he or she "owns." This can be a slave, a ward, or a consanguineous descendant. Usually it is a low-status adolescent (S.L.G.A., General Minute Papers 842 [1903]; Confidential Minute Papers 3 [1903]; Court Record Book, Moyamba District, May 1901–September 1903; March 1910–May 1911). Kopytoff and Miers have clearly described the way in which members of African corporate descent groups "belong" to the group as members and as part of its wealth (1977:10). With cannibalism one eats what one is attached to. Sherbros say human flesh is attractively "sweet," a polysemic term meaning that which gives pleasure in a personal sensuous way. It is used as a reference of genuine endearment to children and lovers, as well as to food. These meanings of "owning" and "eating" are profoundly ambivalent.

Cannibalism beliefs are of course linked to witchcraft beliefs, and archival testimonies as well as ethnographic conversations are quite explicit about the possibility of witches transforming themselves into leopards or crocodiles, killing and "eating" in the dark of night or hidden under water (S.L.G.A., Native Affairs Minute Paper 118 [1882] and 818 [1890]; Opinion Book [1886]). Descriptions of Leopard Society gatherings and feasts indicate they are held in the forest, not in the village (MacCormack [Notebook] 1976:105, 518–519). They are a nighttime activity. Often there is genuine ambiguity about the nature of Leopard or Alligator, as in this account from a Native Affairs Minute Paper of 1890: "I cannot tell whether the things I saw were persons or beasts. I believe that the things . . . were Human Leopards. By Human Leopards I mean people who turn themselves into Leopards" (S.L.G.A., Paper 436). Thus ambiguities in a *social* dimension are reflected in the ambiguity of *symbolic* representations. People seem unsure about whether the manifestations are animal (and can be killed and eaten with impunity) or human (and embedded within moral social networks).

Clearly, the distinguishing activity of Leopards and Alligators is to "eat," another polysemic term in Sherbro thought. When the Poro or Thoma societies begin an initiation season, the great spirit of the forest begins to "eat," taking initiates into the initiation grove (MacCormack 1981:102). The spirit has mouth, gut, and vagina in a single passage, which transforms protosocial children into responsible adults with a new social identity at the conclusion of initiation rites. People even speak of a political figure or the head of a cooperative who "eats" the money entrusted to him; the money can never be recovered. In these contexts, eating means an *irreversible* transformation in which there can never be a return to things as they were before. In socially constructive initiation rituals, the initiates' social identity is altered, but their individual identity is still intact; it still maintains continuity. In antisocial cannibal societies, or with the predations of wild carnivores, the individual who is eaten does not gain an enhanced social identity but is obliterated. (When slaves are eaten by cannibals, they are persons without descendants [Mac-Cormack 1977:188] and would not even be ritually remembered after death.) Symbolic "eating" in initiation rituals is a process for creating a strong, socially responsible *society*. Physical "eating" in cannibal societies is a process for achieving strong-willed *individuals*.

COGNITIVE STRUCTURE

The Thoma society, a legitimate Sherbro sodality, uses animal categories in the context of initiation rites. The first pair of masks to appear on the ritual stage are the dwarf duiker and the dwarf hippopotamus. The duiker, a small antelope, is a forest mammal, a benign vegetarian, in contrast to the "cannibalistic" leopard. The latter is not represented by a mask, but the contrast is of such general knowledge it does not need to be spelled out concretely. The duiker in Sherbro oral literature is a well-mannered trickster who mediates forces in nature and humanlike society to get a spouse, children, food, and other valued things. The hippopotamus is a water animal, a benign vegetarian, in contrast to the "cannibalistic" crocodile. The latter is not represented in mask, but is the well-known contrastive animal. Duiker and hippopotamus are the first pair of masks to appear in initiation ritual. They symbolize the idea that "wild" unsocialized children are being transformed into cultured adults, but will retain some of the fertile vigor of the animal world.

This pair of animal masks is supplanted in the ritual process by a male-female pair of humanoid masks. They appear at the climax of the initiation ritual, when the ancestors have been well "fed" with libations and offerings of cooked animal and vegetable food. The final ritual pair to appear are the living male and female co-heads of the Thoma society.

On the overt, normative level, mundane farmers and fishers, members of Poro, Sande, or Thoma, are socially constructive members of the "commonwealth," diurnally active, and on the "white" side of society. Hippopotamus and duiker are pure animal, vegetarian, and diurnal; they are unambiguously benign. But there is the dark zone of nocturnally active Human Leopards and Crocodiles who are neither purely human nor purely animal. However, recall my earlier comment that if you choose your informants carefully, and feed this model back to them, they will agree on the normative level, but pragmatically hint that even respected leaders get power by dark means. People cross back and forth between whiteness and blackness throughout their lives. Deep within all of us is both white and black. Ambiguity is the ultimate truth.

	WATER	LAND	
Human	Fishermen (Poro, Sande, Thoma)	Farmers (Poro, Sande, Thoma)	Benign, socially constructive "eaters"
	Witches and those who selfishly seek power		
Ambiguous	Human Alligators	Human Leopards	Selfish hidden "eaters"
Animal	Crocodile	Leopard	
	Hippopotamus	Duiker	Benign "eaters"

CONCLUSION

To conclude, animals are eaten and eaters. In a well-known phrase, they are not only good to eat, but good to think, as we have seen. But pushing beyond cognitive analysis into affect, people who either are transformed witches, or are dressed to resemble leopards or crocodiles, clearly intimidate others in contests of political will. For example, in 1917, Paramount Chief Bai Sherbro was accused by his political enemies of being a cannibal and the head of the Alligator society. The District Commissioner thought of calling the whole chiefdom together to decide if the chief should be deposed (S.L.G.A., Confidential Minute Paper 163 [1917]). In other cases, the Paramount Chief's political rivals, or even "strangers" who had migrated into the area to trade, becoming rich and arrogant against established authority, were accused. They were reported by the Paramount Chief to be cannibals, and, in the first case, the Governor authorized the Paramount Chief to punish his political rivals (S.L.G.A., Native Affairs Department Letterbook, December 27, 1893). In the second case, the District Commissioner had the "strangers" deported (S.L.G.A., Colonial Secretary's Office,

Judicial Proceedings, May 1931). On another occasion, people made leopard noises around the house of the District Commissioner himself until he left town, only to return with a detachment of soldiers who found nothing (S.L.G.A., Criminal Court Record, Bonthe, 1909).

There was a considerable spate of cannibal accusations at the end of the 19th century and early 20th century when colonial rule was imposed. There was another spate in the 1930s when the economy was affected by a world depression. In the early 20th century, the following disruptions to the area occurred.

1. British colonial authority was being imposed on the Protectorate.

2. A house tax was levied.

3. Chiefs were being denied many of their prerogatives, including tribute and court fees.

4. The local economy was disrupted by talk of abolishing domestic slavery, accomplished in 1927.

5. Chiefdom boundaries were being drawn on maps.

6. Migrating traders came in, seeking broker roles and even political prerogatives.

7. Trade wars, including slave raiding, were commonplace.

Since independence, the same idiom of political expression persists. It can be used to menace people, a technique for intimidating and controlling a rival political faction. For example, in late 1976, shortly before disorder throughout the country caused the government to dissolve parliament and call elections, I talked with three people who had been harassed by those they identified as Human Leopards. This was in a local area I knew well. One person was a strong-willed and outspoken relative of a powerful political figure. She had been walking along a deserted path when a man, scantily clad, leapt from the forest (bush fallow). Although only one man threatened to "catch" her, all the bush around was shaking, indicating that there were many others, each shaking a sapling. The rivalry between this woman's relative and another powerful political figure from the same local area was being expressed in power plays at the national level and by the mobilization of groups of kin and clients at the local level. The tensions later erupted into real violence in the local constituency after elections were called.

But overt violence is uncommon in this area, and just the accusation of cannibalism continues to be a strong political weapon. Chiefs, government officials, and allegedly even a prime minister have been brought down by accusations of cannibalism. It is a way of saying: "This person is a willful, selfish seeker after antisocial personal power, and not fit to rule."

REFERENCES

FYFE, CHRISTOPHER. 1962. *A History of Sierra Leone.* Oxford: Oxford University Press.
KALOUS, MILAN. 1974. *Cannibals and Tongo Players of Sierra Leone.* Auckland: Wright and Carman Ltd.
KOPYTOFF, IGOR, and SUZANNE MIERS. 1977. Introduction. *Slavery in Africa* (S. Miers and I. Kopytoff, eds.), pp. 3–84. Madison: University of Wisconsin Press.
LITTLE, KENNETH. 1965. The Political Function of the Poro, Part I. *Africa* 35:349–365.
_____. 1966. The Political Function of the Poro, Part II. *Africa* 36:62–71.
MacCORMACK, CAROL P. (HOFFER). 1972. Mende and Sherbro Women in High Office. *Canadian Journal of African Studies* 2:151–164.
_____. 1974. Madam Yoko: Ruler of the Kpa Mende Confederacy. *Woman, Culture and Society* (M. Z. Rosaldo and L. Lamphere, eds.), pp. 173–188. Stanford: Stanford University Press.
_____. 1977. Wono: Institutionalized Dependency in Sherbro Descent Groups. *Slavery in Africa* (S. Miers and I. Kopytoff, eds.), pp. 181–204. Madison: University of Wisconsin Press.
_____. 1979. Sande: The Public Face of a Secret Society. *The New Religions of Africa* (B. Jules-Rosette, ed.), pp. 27–37. Norwood, N.J.: Ablex Press.
_____. 1980. Proto-Social to Adult: A Sherbro Transformation. *Nature, Culture and Gender* (C. P. MacCormack and M. Strathern, eds.), pp. 95–118. Cambridge: Cambridge University Press.
RODNEY, WALTER. 1970. *A History of the Upper Guinea Coast 1545–1800.* Oxford: Oxford University Press.
SIERRA LEONE GOVERNMENT ARCHIVES. Specific citations given in the text.

Cannibalism and Arapesh Cosmology

A Wartime Incident with the Japanese

DONALD TUZIN

The Ilahita Arapesh inhabit seven large, sedentary villages in the lower Torricelli foothills and upper plains of the East Sepik Province in northeastern New Guinea.[1] A predominantly horticultural people, the Arapesh have customarily dined on yam, taro, sago, banana, a variety of other lowland tropical plants, and, with much less regularity, animal flesh. There is no hard evidence that they have ever made a practice of eating one another; neither, it appears, have any of their immediate neighbors ever indulged in cannibalism. How, then, does it happen that the *image* of cannibalism—openly expressed or thinly veiled—recurs with sufficient prominence and frequency to qualify it as an object of fascination for

[1] Research was conducted in Ilahita village during 21 months in the period 1969-1972, with major funding granted by the Research School of Pacific Studies, Australian National University, and with a supplementary grant-in-aid from the Wenner-Gren Foundation for Anthropological Research. The author is grateful to these organizations and to the following individuals for their valuable comments and criticisms on an earlier version of this paper: John W. Connor, George DeVos, Benjamin Kilborne, Eugene Kumekawa, Michael E. Meeker, Edward Norbeck, Robert J. Smith, Melford E. Spiro, Marc J. Swartz, and the members of the anthropology seminar, University of Sydney.

DONALD TUZIN is Professor of Anthropology at the University of California, San Diego.

these people? If, as Susanne Langer says (1953:390), all knowledge goes back to experience, then how can it be said that the Arapesh understanding of "cannibalism" has a basis in their experience? In this paper I will suggest that the answers to these questions constitute a basis for interpreting the significance of this symbolic figure within the Arapesh cosmological scheme. Briefly stated, my interpretation is that the image of "cannibalism" is, inter alia, a device through which the unthinkable (eating people) gives form to the otherwise inconceivable substance of the relationship to oneself and to the supernatural. Paradoxically, then, the symbolic office of cannibalism depends upon its being thought of as "unthinkable."

The problem of symbolic interpretation is perhaps most efficiently. approached by tracing the imprint that cultural predispositions have made on the Arapesh response to two fairly recent encounters with actual cannibalism. This will provide an analytic template which, in a later paper, can be applied to the more difficult task of understanding the genesis and maintenance of the predisposition itself. Let me begin with the more straightforward of the two instances.

In the late 1930s, Australian pacification of the area was only starting, but there was a sufficient police presence to enable a few of the more daring young men to undertake the adventure of indenturing themselves as laborers on the coastal and island copra and coca plantations. Far from home in such places as New Britain, New Ireland, and the Madang area, workers from the Sepik basin tended to associate with one another as compatriots, and thus it was that these Arapesh mingled with eaters of human flesh from the lower Sepik tributaries. Of interest here is not so much the details of the stories they told — and, as graybeards, continue to tell — as it is their general attitude toward cannibalism and other exotic practices which allegedly exist among these distant Sepik and other foreign peoples. This may be characterized as an amused, faintly condescending interest that is morally neutral in tone. Extreme cultural relativists, my informants find nothing provocative in such faraway customs, and often they dismiss the whole matter by pronouncing that those Sepiks are "another kind of man"; if they choose to eat each other, that is their business. In other words, cultural and geographical remoteness fosters a remoteness to consciousness as well: however normal cannibalism may be to some peoples, it has nothing to do with us. This remoteness, and its correspondingly in-different attitude, should be kept in mind while we consider the second instance, in which cannibalism occurred literally and figuratively much closer to home.

During the opening weeks of 1945, some Arapesh individuals—it is not known precisely how many—fell victim to cannibalism perpetrated by Japanese troops garrisoned in the villages of the region. Units of the beleaguered 18th Army, the Japanese had been sent there six months previously to forage off the gardens—this in response to General Douglas MacArthur's forces having cut their overseas supply lines. The evidence that they committed cannibalism consists of reliable eyewitness accounts given to me in the field and later confirmed by officers' battle diaries housed in the Australian war archives, in which references are made to unmistakable physical evidence discovered in the packs of slain Japanese soldiers.[2] Upon first hearing of this, I suggested to my informants—one of whom, from hiding, had seen his father eaten—that the starving may resort to extreme measures in order to survive; but this construction was emphatically rejected. It is not true, the villagers insisted, that the Japanese were starving; on the contrary, there was an abundance of garden produce. Why then, I asked, would they have done it? My informants responded that they had been driven to it by fear: aware of their imminent annihilation by vastly superior Australian forces that were sweeping the region, these desperate men became deranged and turned to cannibalism as the ultimate, anguished abandonment of their humanity. They became, in a word, deculturated: the resort to cannibalism was the surest sign that they had madly embraced the chaos that lay before them.

We may never know the full circumstances surrounding this grim episode. The evidence indicates, however, that the Arapesh interpretation, while ingenious and probably correct to some extent, reveals more about their symbolic understandings of cannibalism than it does about the real reasons behind the Japanese acts. The soldiers certainly had cause to be frightened, perhaps desperately so.

---

[2] Numerous additional references to cannibalism by Japanese troops in Melanesia (including the East Sepik area) and the Philippines are to be found in the extensive archives and histories arising out of the war-crimes inquiries commissioned by Australia and the United States immediately after the war.

Demoralized, sick and weakened, low on medicine and ammunition, their hinterland haven was turning into a death trap: by official counts, the killed-to-captured ratio among the Japanese was 33:1, while the Australians were experiencing an almost trivial number of casualties. Furthermore, having for months enjoyed close affection and hospitality from their indigenous hosts, the garrison was now suffering harassment and ambush from villagers who had deserted to the forest and were now actively collaborating with the advancing Australians. As Lieutenant-General Kane Yoshiwara wrote after the war (Long 1963:306):

Once the natives knew where we were . . . they induced aircraft to strafe and bomb us. In addition the natives in the rear rebelled and losses were caused among those of our men who were employed on liaison or food gathering.[3]

Granting the distressing hopelessness of their situation, is it credible that these seasoned troops, veterans of Salamaua and other bloody campaigns, were so driven by fear as to abandon the last vestige of their humanity? Perhaps. But I suggest that a more parsimonious and tenable explanation is precisely the one that my informants were so eager to resist, namely, that it was hunger that drove these soldiers to cannibalism.

Consider the following facts, drawn from war records and and from my own ethnographic observations. First, the events in question occurred in February and early March—the preharvest period when, even in normal years, garden food is scarce and the population is forced to subsist mainly on sago flour, a food both difficult to produce and minimal in nutritional value. In that year, the shortage would have been far more acute, since the garrison of several hundred men (in Ilahita village alone) had been in hungry residence for six months. Second, even if any pickings remained in the gardens, under the rapidly deteriorating security conditions it would have been, as Yoshiwara reported, highly dangerous for foraging parties to leave the well-fortified village encampments. Third, the records

---

[3] The "natives in the rear" would have included the Arapesh, who, at this late stage in the local campaign, were engaged in surveillance, sabotage, and minor guerrilla actions on behalf of the Australians. The Arapesh defected because they saw that the Australians were clearly going to win the war, and because they were experiencing increasing brutality, culminating in cannibalism, at the hands of the Japanese.

show that a general directive was issued in February that banned hunting, in order that ammunition could be saved for combat. Against this background there can be little doubt that, regardless of their actual clinical condition, the Japanese perceived themselves to be in critical need of high-quality protein, especially in anticipation of the severe physical demands of combat (cf. Rappaport 1968:84). Finally, on the matter of their mental condition, it must be said that these Japanese, despite being grievously outnumbered and out-gunned, did manage to put up a stiff, well-organized resistance, im-plying that they were not reduced to the demented, panic-stricken state ascribed to them by my informants.

If, as these facts strongly indicate, the resort to cannibalism was a tragic, though entirely rational, act of survival,[4] then the question arises: Why do the Arapesh reject this seemingly obvious explana-tion in favor of the rather baroque and not at all obvious appeal to fear-inspired, deculturated madness? Their reasoning, I suggest, is both culturally and emotionally motivated. The image of "survival cannibalism" is doubly repellent, for it obliterates the cognitive and affective distance which, as we saw, was safely inherent in the Arapesh prospect of cannibalism in other, faraway parts of the Sepik area. To admit that hunger can drive a person to cannibalism is to say that the difference between the cannibal and the noncan-nibal is a matter of degree and circumstance. The unthinkable becomes thinkable, and the imagination is brought within easy reach of a situation in which Ego could become a cannibal or a can-nibal victim.[5] Conversely, it is far more comforting to regard can-

---

[4] The sizable literature on this subject indicates that the motives for Japanese cannibal predation varied considerably, depending on local circumstances and personnel. Published reports, based on interrogation interviews and eyewitness accounts, attribute these practices to epicureanism (Piccigallo 1979:190; Russell 1958:185; Cary 1975:39), madness (Piccigallo 1979:129), the belief that human liver has medicinal and aphrodisiac properties (Cary 1975: 202,210), and the view that black-skinned natives and enemies of the Empire are subhuman (Russell 1958:184). In many of the cases, however, starvation was the precipitating condition. For a novelistic, but highly authentic, account of what happened in the Philippines, see Ooka (1957); see also Ienaga (1978:192).

My primary concern, however, is not to explain why the Japanese did it, but rather to ac-count for why the Arapesh reject the possibility that hunger was involved.

[5] Doubtless, it is the ambiguous allure of this imaginative play, enjoyed in the lardered comfort of one's home, that accounts for the spectacular commercial success of books dealing with cases of survival cannibalism; see, for example, McGlashan (1940), Read (1974), and Stewart (1936). For reasons that will become clear, the Arapesh would find little amusement in such stories.

nibalism as an act of madness — implying motives that are, by definition, unthinkable — or as an act normative within an alien cultural setting which is, itself, unthinkable.

This tendency to mobilize psychocultural defenses in the face of psychoculturally disturbing realities should not appear foreign to us, for it is a common feature of our own strategy for coping with such situations. Many parallel examples could be cited, but the following three should illustrate my point that an image of unthinkability — whatever its particular subject matter may be — is a valuable, sometimes necessary, aid to one's cognitive and emotional equilibrium.

1. For years, medical authorities in the United States have urged the public to regard madness as an "illness," implying that the concondition is, in principle, curable. And yet, although the epithet "crazy" has lost some ground to its humane counterpart "mentally ill," it is clear that ordinary people — and, as one study (Rosenhan 1973) demonstrates, physicians themselves in unguarded moments — continue to perceive insanity to be a qualitatively distinct, spiritually corrupted, and fundamentally irremediable category of existence. The resistance to change stems from the status of the idea as an ancient, deeply embedded metaphor in the language and ideology of our culture, and from the way in which this usage insulates us emotionally from the dreadful implications of mental chaos. Just as the Arapesh are doubly motivated to deny that the Japanese atrocity was a mundane act of survival, so we are doubly motivated to deny that insanity is merely an "illness."

2. The human holocaust engineered by Nazi Germany may be the most disturbing spectacle of our time. The despair of those who attempt to find meaning in it is evident in the bewildered question sometimes asked: How could the people of Goethe and Schiller have done such a thing? I think it is true to say that most people of conscience take a certain grim satisfaction in the view — unquestionable to many — that the Nazi leaders rank among the most monstrous villains of all time. "Inhuman" is the word that comes to mind. For years surrounding his arrest, trial, and execution, Adolph Eichmann epitomized in world opinion all the wickedness of that hideous regime. That this attitude contained elements of the sorts of defenses of which I am speaking, was indicated in the widespread indignation provoked by Hannah Arendt's book *Eichmann in Jerusalem* (1963), subtitled "A Report on the Banality of Evil." This study undermined public defenses by refusing to denounce

Eichmann as a deranged monster: on the contrary, everything about him was banal, humdrum, and frighteningly ordinary. And the true horror of his evil, Arendt thoughtfully concluded, lay in the painful fact that it, too, was banal, thinkable, and well within the possibilities of human experience. The anxieties evoked by this revelation need no further comment.

3. As a final illustration, one which touches on our own attitudes toward cannibalism, consider the well-known incident from Greek mythology in which Atreus dealt a gory reprisal on his brother Thyestes for having seduced his wife. The revenge was that Atreus, concealing his knowledge of the offense, invited Thyestes to a banquet and served him the flesh of his own (Thyestes') sons as a main course. Now, eating one's own children is an ugly enough prospect; but what adds special poignancy to this story — and perhaps makes us squirm a little in our seats — is that Thyestes did this *unknowingly*. With exquisite economy the myth denies us the comfort of dismissing Thyestes as a lunatic, while at the same time it excites our empathy and anxiety for the purpose of emotionally implicating us in the horror of the deed.

In accord with these illustrations, my argument is that the Arapesh interpretative response to Japanese cannibal predation was a successful attempt to preserve the defensive distancing that is intrinsic to their traditional, culturally constituted image of cannibalism. That is to say, they prevented the unthinkable from becoming thinkable. To adopt a phrasing that is only partly metaphorical: rather than facing the horror of a cultural nightmare come true — which is what the idea of survival cannibalism would signify for them — they rationalized the event into a form that could be assimilated to their nightmare and thus enable them to go on dreaming. This brings me to the subject of Arapesh cannibalistic fantasy.

The image of cannibalism operates as a key signifier at every major point in the Arapesh metaphysical scheme; its appearance is an unfailing sign that the context in question is not mundane. Thus, for example, the important myth of Kataomo (see Tuzin 1980: 206–207, 332–334) characterizes the *precultural* condition of the Arapesh as a time when exchange partners gave each other a son and a daughter to eat. The story tells how one pair of victims escaped this fate, grew to adulthood while in hiding, and eventually returned to their home with the civilizing gift of pig flesh. Similarly, in various legends and horror stories the *extracultural* condition of anthropomorphic demons and ogres is signified by the claim that they feed on human flesh, either through their mouth or (in the case of female demons) their anus. In the *postcultural* scheme, ghosts of the recent dead are imagined to have cannibalistic inclinations toward the living, especially their own children.[6] And again, witches, who are always male, qualify for admission to the *decultural* domain by virtue of having partaken of human flesh, usually that of an infant or child.[7] Finally, the *supracultural* spirits that preside over the men's cult are presumed to eat, by mysterious and invisible means, the bodies of enemy dead and human sacrificial victims. Since the cessation of these sanguinary customs, it is alleged that the cult spirits have begun feasting in earnest on their own people, with the result that, now, many routine deaths in the village are colored with cannibalistic overtones (Tuzin 1980:288). Although the connection between ancestral and cult spirits is only vaguely conceived, there is considerable evidence that the relationship is one of mutual identity.

In sum, this metaphysical system construes Arapesh culture to be an island of civilization surrounded on all sides by more or less constantly menacing man-eaters. The unthinkability of cannibalism thus serves as a synecdoche for the unthinkability of the metaphysical domains to which it belongs. To recognize that cannibalism can be thinkable as a mundane act of survival would be to induce the nightmarish ruination of the structure of ideas in terms of which Arapesh culture identifies and knows itself. Hence the villagers' motivation to assign the Japanese deed to a category (the "deculturated") that is familiar and thus cognitively manageable.

But nightmares, whatever cognitive elements they contain, are better known for their emotional potency, and so it is necessary to consider the affective side of the Arapesh response. This may be ap-

---

[6] In one particularly graphic horror story, the devouring rage of the ghost is triggered by the extravagant sexuality of his son and daughter-in-law displayed in the presence of his (the dead father's) skull.

[7] Although certain self-acclaimed witches had confided to me that they had done this, my inclination was to discount these statements as empty, perverse boasts. Then, on one occasion, a bereaved young father, yielding to mission pressure, decided to forego the usual precaution of guarding his baby's grave. That night, the grave was robbed. One must draw the dismal conclusion that in a society which holds that the act of cannibalism confers unlimited power on the actor, there will be no shortage of persons willing to try.

proached by asking the obvious question: In view of the vast cultural, racial, and linguistic gulf separating them from the Japanese, why did the Arapesh not simply dismiss the whole problem of meaning with the same relative indifference they apply to the notion of cannibalism among distant Sepik groups? One answer, of course, is that it is not so easy to maintain equanimity when it is one's own kith and kin who are being eaten. More significantly, however, having hosted these soldiers for the preceding six months, the villagers knew very well that this cannibalism was a grotesque abberation of their normal and approved mode of behavior. For the same reason, my informants could not bring themselves to condemn their predators as monstrous butchers and ghouls—and herein lies the true heart of this tragedy. The fact is, despite the record of atrocities, nearly everyone with whom I spoke remembered the Japanese with palpable warmth and affection. One informant, who had been a child at the time, broke into tears as he recalled the kindly young soldier who had lived with his family and had taken him by the hand to the gardens each day—the kindly young soldier who, he added bitterly, did not deserve to die in a rain of Australian bombs. Most of the Japanese, it appears, were virtually adopted into the families with which they were quartered.

Against this background of mutual trust and affection, we can begin to appreciate the nightmarish aura that arose when the Japanese turned to cannibalism. For it was in this event that personal and cultural horror intersected. Most of the instances of mythic and ritual fantasy mentioned earlier highlight the theme of parents or parent-figures devouring their children. While it is difficult to argue conclusively that the Arapesh identified the Japanese specifically as father-figures, the recollections I recorded amply disclose that the relationship contained much that is reminiscent of filial sentiment. In addition, it is plain that the Arapesh looked up to the Japanese as protectors and providers: the soldiers initially announced themselves to be liberators from Euro-Australian tyranny, and given the minimal and somewhat checkered history of outside contact until that time (Tuzin 1976:25–27), the villagers had no reason to disbelieve them; the Arapesh credit the Japanese with putting an end to intervillage warfare, and it is true that the area enjoyed unprecedented peace during the early phase of the occupation; finally, the Japanese introduced several new cultigens, including sweet potato (*Ipomoea* spp.), and tried to find ways of improving the productivity of native horticulture, thus partaking of the nutritive role that is so much a hallmark of Arapesh parenthood (cf. Mead 1950: 69). Thus it happened that the shattering, personal betrayal involved in the Japanese predation brought to life the age-old phantasm of Arapesh nightmare: the cannibal-parent—the parent who feeds you, but for whom you become food (Devereux 1980). But the Arapesh successfully denied that the phantasm *had* come to life. For, rather than succumb to the horrid fact that the Japanese had killed and eaten them *simply because they were hungry*, the Arapesh found refuge in the comforting, culturally available idea that the deed was a fear-inspired act of deculturated madness and was, after all, unthinkable.[8]

Returning to the question posed at the beginning of this essay, the Arapesh knowledge of cannibalism is indeed rooted in their experience, but in a complex way. The only direct knowledge they have stems from their scary experience with the Japanese. And yet, ironically, that encounter did not teach them anything about cannibalism that they did not already know, since their interpretation of the episode was entirely prefigured by a deeper kind of knowledge that is codified in a variety of cultural fantasies and ideas. The experience that certifies that deeper knowledge is partly to be found in the oral-aggressive fantasies of early childhood (Sagan 1974), operating in probable conjunction with certain neurological associations detectable between eating and emotionality (Tuzin 1978). More specific to the Arapesh case, however, is the portentous fact that their traditional subsistence pattern entailed rare but intense periods of famine. Like the Goodenough Islanders, the Arapesh may well have reason to know and fear "that terrible symbol of cultural suicide, the eating of children" (Young 1971:188). Pending a more extensive inquiry, I hope that this essay has achieved the modest goal of demonstrating that, for the Arapesh, "cannibalism"

---

[8] According to Professor Peter Lawrence (personal communication), tne Ngaing of the Rai Coast were quite matter-of-fact in their assertion that the Japanese garrisoned in their area ate people because they were hungry. The crucial difference between the Ngaing and the Arapesh is that the former had been, until recently, cannibals themselves! For the Ngaing cannibalism, far from being unthinkable, was almost commonplace; and this is why they (and not the Arapesh) were able to see the Japanese act for what is was. I am indebted to Professor Lawrence for this most valuable comparative insight.

is an image of unthinkability par excellence and that, as such, its symbolic office is to call forth those metaphysical categories of which, from time to time, people stand in great need.

REFERENCES

ARENDT, HANNAH.   1963.   *Eichmann in Jerusalem: A Report on the Banality of Evil.* New York: Viking Press.

CARY, OTIS, ed.   1975.   *War-Wasted Asia: Letters, 1945–46.* Tokyo: Kodansha International.

DEVEREUX, GEORGE.   1980.   The Cannibalistic Impulses of Parents. *Basic Problems of Ethnopsychiatry* (G. Devereux), pp. 122–137. Chicago: University of Chicago Press.

IENAGA, SABURO.   1978.   *The Pacific War, 1931–1945: A Critical Perspective on Japan's Role in World War II.* New York: Pantheon Books.

LANGER, SUSANNE.   1953.   *Feeling and Form.* New York: Scribner's.

LONG, GAVIN.   1963.   *The Final Campaigns (Australia in the War of 1939–1945,* ser. 1, vol. 7). Canberra: Australian War Memorial.

McGLASHAN, C. F.   1940.   *History of the Donner Party: A Tragedy of the Sierra.* Stanford, Calif.: Stanford University Press.

MEAD, MARGARET.   1950.   *Sex and Temperament in Three Primitive Societies.* New York: Mentor.

OOKA, SHOHEI.   1957.   *Fires on the Plain.* New York: Knopf.

PICCIGALLO, PHILIP R.   1979.   *The Japanese on Trial: Allied War Crimes Operations in the East, 1945–1951.* Austin: University of Texas Press.

RAPPAPORT, ROY A.   1968.   *Pigs for the Ancestors: Ritual in the Ecology of a New Guinea People.* New Haven: Yale University Press.

READ, PIERS PAUL.   1974.   *Alive: The Story of the Andes Survivors.* Philadelphia: Lippincott.

ROSENHAN, D. L.   1973.   On Being Sane in Insane Places. *Science* 179:250–258.

RUSSELL, LORD OF LIVERPOOL.   1958.   *The Knights of Bushido: The Shocking History of Japanese War Atrocities.* New York: Berkeley.

SAGAN, ELI.   1974.   *Cannibalism: Human Aggression and Cultural Form.* New York: Harper & Row.

STEWART, GEORGE R.   1936.   *Ordeal by Hunger: The Story of the Donner Party.* Boston: Houghton Mifflin.

TUZIN, DONALD F.   1976.   *The Ilahita Arapesh: Dimensions of Unity.* Berkeley: University of California Press.

————.   1978.   Sex and Meat-Eating in Ilahita: A Symbolic Study. *Canberra Anthropology* 1:82–93.

————.   1980.   *The Voice of the Tambaran: Truth and Illusion in Ilahita Arapesh Religion.* Berkeley: University of California Press.

YOUNG, MICHAEL W.   1971.   *Fighting with Food: Leadership, Values and Social Control in a Massim Society.* London: Cambridge University Press.

Raw Women, Cooked Men, and Other "Great Things" of the Fiji Islands

MARSHALL SAHLINS

Cannibalism among this people is one of their institutions; it is interwoven in the elements of society; it forms one of their pursuits and is regarded by the mass as a refinement. [Reverend Thomas Williams, *Fiji and the Fijians*, 1859]

Traditional Fijian myths about the origin of cannibalism are rarely found. Perhaps because the story, once told, tells all. The origin of cannibalism is the origin of culture.[1]

The "first man" lives alone with his aging wife and three daughters near Vatukarasa, on the western coast of Viti Levu [location specified in marginal note]. The old man broods on killing his wife and replacing her with his daughters, there being no one else to marry them. But one day the daughters find a handsome young

---

[1] The myth herein presented in synoptic form is the most detailed account of the origin of cannibalism I have been able to discover: a 19th-century English-language text included among the papers of Sir Arthur Gordon (Stanmore Collection), first Governor of the Colony of Fiji (1875-1879). The text, together with commentary and marginal notes, appears to be in the hand of Gordon's personal assistant, Edward O'Brien Heffernan. Other notices of the beginnings of cannibalism are more schematic, but likewise and generally entail the idea that it was not an original trait, having come to Fiji with belligerent immigrants and/or chiefs, who also brought constant warfare (Pritchard 1968[1866]:381-382; Rokowaqa n.d.:42; Thompson 1940:103; but see Waterhouse 1866:312). Cannibalism is thus ascribed to the elementary Fijian opposition between immigrant warrior chiefs and the indigenous "people of the land," who are by nature peaceable cultivators (cf. Sahlins 1981).

MARSHALL SAHLINS is Professor of Anthropology at the University of Chicago.

stranger washed up on the shore from the wreck of his canoe. They restore the half-drowned castaway and suggest he take them as wives. The stranger agrees and accordingly requests the daughters of their father, offering in return to plant the elder's food. Deeming the proposal impudent and the offer insufficient, however, the old man turns the youth out, saying he will have to do a work of *mana*[2] to merit the daughters. The disconsolate hero, whose name [we now learn] is Tabua, "Whale Tooth," sleeps fitfully and next morning eats some Tahitian chestnuts and a snake he has managed to kill. Suddenly he remembers having seen a whale drift ashore the same time he did, and realizing the people here are still ignorant of whale teeth, he invents a disingenuous scheme to demonstrate his *mana*. In the difficult task of extracting the dead whale's teeth, however, he accidently knocks out four of his own front teeth. Still, he is able to fit the accident into his plan. He burns the whale carcass and returns after some days to the house of the "first man," whom he finds lecturing his daughters on the fickleness of youth, and proposing that his wife be strangled and they take her place. To the elder's chagrin, Tabua proceeds to tell a fabricated story about the whale teeth, a myth within the myth: that he had cleared some forest in the manner of a yam garden, and planted his own four teeth, which in the course of eight days miraculously increased in number and size. The self-evident value of the whale teeth allows the ruse to succeed. Indeed, the evidence of Tabua's feat so delights the mother and daughters that they fall gleefully on the elder, in the course of which embrace his wife pulls out his beard. The old man reluctantly consents to his daughters' marriage, claiming in return the right to make certain laws: that hereafter whale teeth shall be called *"tabua"* after the hero's name; that such *tabua* shall be used as payment for the woman in marriage; and that all further castaways who wash ashore be killed and eaten, lest they, like Tabua's teeth, should only increase in the land. Hence the title of this tale, "How the Fijians first became cannibals."[3]

The etiological myths and historical practices of Fijian cannibalism interpret each other. The ground of their mutual intelligibility is a system of relationships among persons and the objects of their existence. Indeed the action of the person Tabua in the myth is the function of the object *tabua* (the whale tooth) in life.

Whale teeth are Fiji's supreme riches. The whale tooth, says the Fijian sage Ratu Deve Toganivalu (*Ms.*), is used to kill men, to make war, to supplicate *(sorova)* the chief or the god and to fetch the woman in marriage *(duguca na yalewa)*. Hence Commodore Wilkes's observation: "A whale's tooth is about the price of a human life" (1845, v.

[2] The English text reads "perform a miracle," quite probably a translation of the Fijian *cakamana,* "to do *mana,*" "to make *mana,*" "to work *mana.*"

[3] A striking permutation of the same myth and themes occurs in the Maori story of Tini-rau and Kae (White 1887–1890, v.2:127ff.).

3:90). I stress the role of whale teeth as starting gifts of marriage and of assassinations or wars whose proximate goal is the acquisition of sacrificial cum cannibal victims. An initial prestation of *tabua* to the father of the prospective bride "cuts" (*musaka*) her from her natal kin. Gifts of whale teeth mobilize allied lands for war, or send the ritual assassin on his fatal mission, even as successful man-slayers are again rewarded by this greatest of treasures (*i yau tālei, kāmunaga*). So in the myth, the hero named Whale Tooth is able to found a society in which the capture of foreign victims compensates for the surrender of native women, thus creating an ordered circulation of the principal sources of social reproduction. The myth is about the origins of exogamy, the incest tabu, riches, and bridewealth, as well as cannibalism—cannibalism in fact is the most obscure part of it. That it was all brought about by the *mana* of a ruse means many things: perhaps among them that the *mana* of the social contract lies in symbolism itself (cf. Valeri, in press).

As an object or being from beyond society that is able to generate its main relationships, the whale tooth is in such (Durkheimian) respects divine.[4] Hence Hocart's analysis of its economic value: "A few ounces of divinity were worth pounds of gross matter" (Hocart 1969b:101)—an observation that goes a long way toward explaining Fijian demand-functions in the important trade in whale teeth with Tongans and Europeans during the 19th century.[5] In the same respects, whale teeth are like chiefs, also strangers from overseas

[4] For Durkheim (1947), "god" is the way people figure to themselves the constraints and satisfactions of society, thus, a displaced representation of the social totality. I am here suggesting a slight elaboration of the idea. What is truly powerful are things and beings that are able to subsist beyond the bounds of a society which for ordinary men is the necessary condition of their existence. Moreover, it would only be from this transcendental position that god could make society. This helps explain many Fijian things, such as why the hunting of whales is unthinkable to the people (Wilkes 1845, v.3:194), the divine efficacy of the *tabua* (whale tooth) being inconsistent with human control and production. Or again the association—widespread in the Austronesian family—between the divine and the natural (and/or the foreign), as opposed to the human and the cultural. And finally, then, the appreciation in value of whale teeth according to their appearance of use and age: appearance that is the sign and summation in concrete qualities of the social relations the *tabua* have constituted—the men killed, the women married, the alliances made and unmade, the victories and the submissions.

[5] On the role of whale teeth in 19th-century commerce, see, for example, Lockerby et al. (1925:25, 112), Jackson (in Erskine 1967[1853]:25-112), Quain (1948:21-22), Wilkes (1845, v.3:220,357).

who synthesize the elementary oppositions of social and cosmic order, and are known in their own right as "gods" *(kalou)*. It follows that Tabua of the myth is a chief, just as in life the whale tooth is a "chiefly thing" *(ka vakaturaga)*.[6]

Tabua will marry the daughters and sire the successors of "the first man." The myth places itself within the classic Fijian (indeed Austronesian) opposition between an intrusive foreign nobility and the "indigenous people" or "native owners" of the soil *(i taukei)*. "The chiefs . . . came from overseas," Hocart was told by an Oneata man; "it is so in all countries of Fiji" (1929:129; cf. Sahlins 1981). So the native owners are also called "the land" or "land people" *(na vanua, kai vanua)*, and are said to be gifted farmers, in contrast to immigrants such as the chief who came by sea. The chief is *kai tani*, a "different person" from the people he rules. He is their divine "guest" or *vulagi*, a term Hocart glosses as "heavenly god." Myths and genealogies also attest that throughout maritime Fiji the advent of the stranger-king is marked by his appropriation of a ranking woman (or women) of the indigenous people—or, more abstractly, by his appropriation of the land's reproductive powers. In the documented historical parallels, a vanquished people submit to their conquerer by presenting to him a basket of earth (the land) and daughters of their own chief (e.g., Cargill 1977:160; Hunt *Ms.:* Journal, Oct. 29, 1840; Williams 1931:226). Usurpation is the first principle of political legitimacy. But in history as well as myth, the usurper will provide human sacrificial victims in return: cooked men for the raw women (i.e., virgin daughters).

A passage in the 1840 journal of the admirable missionary-ethnographer John Hunt describes an incident that could be appended to the myth of Tabua as a logical consequence (*Ms.:* Journal, Feb. 11, 1840). Tui Cakau, paramount of Cakaudrove, is distributing 11 rebel corpses for his people's consumption. "The king himself made a speech," writes Hunt, "a very rare thing; he only speaks [in

---

[6] In Lekutu, Vanua Levu, a certain whale tooth is the palladium of the chiefdom. It has the same title (Tu Lekutu) as the ruling chief; whoever holds it receives the tributes of first-fruits (Quain 1948:189ff., 224; cf. Hocart 1952:201). Many Fijian lands *(vanua)* had a "state basket" *(kato ni tu)*, holding the treasures in whale teeth received by the chief from dealings with other lands (Hocart 1929:209; *FN:*2365-2366; *HF* [re Bau]). Again in chants *(meke)* there are frequent metaphoric associations between ruling chiefs and whale teeth, as in the famous lament of the Lau paramount wherein his body is likened to "the skin of the whale tooth" *(kuli ni tabua)*.

ceremonies] when whale teeth are divided or the bodies of men. These are their two great things." Brother Hunt here adopts Fijian idiom. "Great thing" (*ka levu*) is what they say—yet not of whale teeth or cannibal victims only. Also of the chief himself.[7] "The Great Thing" (*Na Kalevu*) is indeed the title of the most powerful chief in western Fiji, head of the Nadroga confederacy (the very setting of the myth of Tabua, supposing Heffernan's marginal note concerning Vatukarasa is correct). And the legend of the latest Nadroga dynasty is another version of the same myth. A handsome young stranger from Tonga is washed up on the beach near Sigatoka just as the Nadroga people are about to install their own native chief. Dazzled by the stranger's appearance, the elders decide to invest him in place of the would-be successor. Along with the chiefdom, the stranger-king is ceded 100 wives, one from each subordinate village (Hocart *FN:* 2750–2753).

In a parallel tale from nearby Noikoro (Brewster *Ms.*) the foreign hero marries the native chief's daughter to give rise to the present ruling lineage (*mataqali*) called "The Sharks" (*Na Qio*). It is all as in the Hawaiian proverb, "A chief is a shark who travels on the land" (Handy and Pukui 1972:199). The suggestion, upon which I shall proceed to expound, is that the stranger's powers are in fact terrible. He is by nature a ferocious cannibal. But he will be induced to satisfy his appetites in the metaphoric mode of "consuming" the woman, taking her sexually (cf. Quain 1948:322), and end by feeding the people instead of eating them.

I refer to the Lau Islands of eastern Fiji, where the theory of chiefship is characteristically more explicit, and connects on from legend to known practices of royal violence. Tui Lakeba, or The-Slayer-Who-Came-from-Heaven, destroys all the native gods/chiefs of mainland Fiji and, having stolen the first-fruit tributes of the Lau rulers, also makes them his cannibal fare (Fison 1904). But Tui Lakeba spares the autochthonous snake-god of Fiji, the creator Degei, and encompasses his descent instead by marrying his daughter, who bears Tui Lakeba the heir to the Lau chiefship. And whereas the western chiefs who drift ashore, such as Tabua, are kinless, the chiefs of the East and the Islands demonstrate their

---

[7] Hocart's informant, taking him to see the ruling chief of Rewa, Roko Tui Dreketi, explains, "We are going to the great thing" *(vua na ka levu*—Hocart *FN:* 2598).

disengagement from the homebred structures of society in more draconic ways. Tui Lakeba threatens to kill his mother and is the dangerous rival of his father, King-of-the-Sky. Likewise, the dynasty of his most recent successors, the Tui Nayau line, begins in legendary feats of parricide and fratricide, a disposition that continued to distinguish the lineage into protohistoric times. "Few high chiefs were not killed," said the Lau nobleman to Hocart (1929:158). The same is truly said of Bau, Rewa, Cakaudrove, and Macuata, to name only the greater chiefdoms whose 19th-century history is notorious for the internal carnage of their royal families.[8]

In the myth of Tabua we find the same themes, except that these western tales tend to be metaphorical where the eastern are often (as genre) historical. Tabua signifies his identity as a cannibal and usurper by his breakfast of snake and *ivi*-nut (Tahitian chestnut). As the snake is the body of the great Degei, by slaying and consuming him the hero is able to incarnate an indigenous divinity. Apparently, he also consumes the daughter, since ancient myth tells that the *ivi*-nut is the form assumed by Degei's female descendants (Rokowaqa, n.d.:5). Eating the snake is thus a mythical representation of what Heusch (1962) calls "the exploit" of the magical king: a victory over the established order that is at the same time a sacrilege. Power reveals and defines itself as a rupture of the people's own moral order. Having committed these monstrous acts against society, proving he is stronger than it, the stranger-king is in a position to constitute it. His advent is a kind of terrible epiphany.

But if the chief comes as a god, we should not forget that (as the missionary says), "their gods are cannibals, like themselves"

---

[8] Reverend Hunt does not entirely exaggerate when he says, "Almost every chief in Feejee feels himself under obligation to be a murderer, and then some other feels himself under the same obligation to murder him" (*Ms.:* Journal, Oct. 29, 1840). In the exploits that marked the beginning of the Tui Nayau dynasty of Lau, a younger brother was first slain by his older brother's son, whereupon the son of the former exacted an equally cruel revenge on both the murderer and his father. The generation of Lau chiefs encountered by the first Methodist missionaries had been earnestly carrying on the lineage tradition. "Brother had murdered brother," said one of Lyth's converts, "until only Malani and Taliai Tupou were left. Then the land had rest." The old folks spoke of one Tahitian chestnut season (i.e., *ivi*, cf. the myth of Tabua) when eight kings were successively installed and murdered (Lyth *Ms.:* "Sketches of John Hunt and Fijian Chiefs"). (For other notices of these struggles see Reid 1977; Hocart *FN:* 2765, 2792, 3155, 3207; Thompson 1940:162.) The famous intrigues and assassinations among the sons of Tabaiwalu in Rewa, contending for the Roko Tui Dreketi title, are documented in Waterhouse (1866:36) and Wilkes (1845, v.3:131). For other areas of Fiji during the same epoch, see, for example, Williams (1859).

(Hazelwood, in Erskine 1967[1853]:24). In this respect, the allusions of the Tabua myth may well be redundant: the hero loses his teeth, the traditional affliction visited upon the crime of endocannibalism, affecting those who eat their own kinsmen, even if unwittingly (Thomson 1968[1908]:102). On the other hand, as the Lau legends would confirm, the marriage of Tabua with the daughters of "the first man" is a domesticated transformation of his cannibal consumption of the indigenous god and his daughters. And here myth again joins custom, since marriage produces the celebrated "sacred nephew" (*vasu*) of Fiji: the sister's son who appropriates and incorporates the privileges of his mother's brother's god.

All this helps explain why Fijians say "the chief is our god" (cf. Hocart 1912:447, 1952:93; Rabuka 1911:156). The paradigmatic privilege of the uterine nephew is to seize (*vasuta*) the offerings made to the god of his mother's brothers (Hocart 1915; 1952:142, 205; cf. Gordon Cumming 1882:165; Wilkes 1845, v. 3:77). It follows that the immigrant chiefs, as wife-takers to the native owners, also take the place of the indigenous god, the one who consumes the sacrifice. Nor is this an occasional or esoteric privilege. It is the global economy of the chiefdom. Before Christianity, all intergroup prestations were formally offered to the god of the recipients, even as their acceptance bestowed life on the givers. Everything we call "trade" and "tribute" was at that time sacrifice. If the goods fell then to the chief of the group that received them it was precisely by his divine right as sister's son, right established through the initial offering of the woman. Hence another of Hocart's memorable dicta: "There is no religion in Fiji, only a system that in Europe has split up into religion and business" (1970[1936]:256).[9]

This also helps account for the distinctive duality of the godhead in traditional Fiji: consisting, on one hand, of the ancient invisible

---

[9] "The people here certainly carry their religion into everything" (Lyth *Ms.*: "Tongan and Fijian Reminiscences"). The formulas of prestation used in great intergroup exchanges (*solevu*) during pre-Christian times make it clear that all these were transactions between gods. Lyth (ibid.) gives an excellent example from Somosomo of calling the shares to the gods, which are then received by their human representatives: "*A 'ena a Loaloa*"—"the [eating-] share of [the god] Loaloa"—"*A sigana a Tavasara*"—"the display/offering of [the god] Tavasara." Thus would the missionaries receive the share of "Jesu Kirisito." Naturally, the prestations of first-fruits were also destined to the god. The form of exchange called *veisā* or trade proper, as of fish for taro between specialized land and sea groups, may have been an exception to this divine economy, as such exchange was not formally handled by "heralds" (*matanivanua*) or priests (*bete*).

gods of the land (*vu/kalou vu*) who governed the fate of the collectivity; and, on the other, their visible instantiations in living chiefs and priests. But the first, the great chiefdom gods, were not the lineage ancestors of the reigning chiefs. Spirits of the original chiefs and/or "sources" (*vu*) of the indigenous lineages, the great gods belonged to the native land people, who accordingly were their priests. During the cult, the indigenous deities became manifest by entering the priest. But otherwise and continuously, they were visibly present in the chief, who, as uterine nephew of their worshippers, had superceded them in this world. Naming the gods of the village temples, the Tamavua chief says, "All these are my names" (Hocart *HF*).[10]

By corollary, god images are absent in traditional Fiji. "They are not idolators," Brother Hunt had to admit, "though they worship false gods, they have no idols" (*Ms.:* Journal, Oct. 28, 1843). Unlike their Tahitian or Hawaiian counterparts, Fijian chiefs and priests did not realize their own divinity by the symbolic associations of a system of human sacrifice designed to bestow life and *mana* on an empirical image, an object which thus assumed, in wood or stone, the alienated form of its victims and suppliants (Valeri, in press). Fijian chiefs and priests were directly consubstantial with the invisible gods by their own substantial consumption of men—if in the mediated, cooked form appropriate to divinity in a mortal frame. Indeed one of the most respectful salutations a lowly commoner could proffer a ruling chief in the political heartlands of southeast Viti Levu was "Eat me!" (Waterhouse 1866:338). And if the feast brought to the chief by a subject people was deemed insufficient, it was only polite form that they offer to include themselves in the repast—"the men are the feast":

A little basket [the feast, of many baskets of food] lies here in the presence of you-

---

[10] It should be observed that all chieftains of land lineages, as well as of superceded chiefly stocks *(malasivo)*, are essentially priests *(bete)*. This would go also for the famous "heralds" or "talking chiefs" *(matanivanua*, "face of the land"). In Rokowaqa's excellent analysis (Rokowaqa, n.d.), heralds are formally referred to as *bete matanivanua*, "priest-heralds." The logic of this is that the heralds stand to and serve the human god, the ruling chief, as the *bete* or priests proper—likewise mouthpieces of the god and mediators between god and people—serve the invisible spirits. The entire organization of the Fijian "land" *(vanua)* was in this decisive respect a ritual congregation, differentiated in lineage *(mataqali)* terms according to the gods served and the services performed.

two [the chief], and a weak branch of a stump [the great kava root] which I put down in the presence of you-two. There is nothing to eat with it. Be gracious; if it is not enough we are its supplement. The men are the feast. [Hocart, *HF:* prestation to the Roko Tui Namata]

Hence the preferential claims of chiefs to enemy bodies and cannibal reputations recorded in contemporary accounts. Moreover, it was god eat god, as in the more legendary chronicles. On the (Polynesian) principle that the offering should be of the nature of the god, the select victims of sacrifice were enemy chiefs and famous warriors. The consecration of the *bakola* to the major war god by chief or priest freed the other bodies taken for more general consumption. According to Reverend Williams, all such consumption was in the nature of communion, since, as he says (1859:194), all *bakola* eaten by men were the food of the gods. Apart from the portions reserved to the sacred chief, the parcels of divine benefit were especially distributed to native chieftains of the land. The logic of the system of sacrifice is thus the same that myth relates as the system of society. In exchange for the raw women originally accorded himself, the immigrant chief provides cooked men.

At this point, it is necessary to provide some descriptive material on the actual practice of cannibalism (cf. Clunie 1977). While cannibal victims (*bakola*) were generally acquired in battle, thus from outside the chiefdom, they might also come from those who had in effect put themselves outside, such as rebellious subjects, or from previously conquered peoples (*qali*). *Bakola* of the latter categories were taken especially for rituals requiring human sacrifice: construction of temples, chiefs' houses, and sacred canoes; ceremonial visits of allied chiefs; installation and first-fruit rites. The ruling chief's special assassins, notably his foreign sailors and turtle-fishers (true "sea people," *kai wai*), were charged with the procurement of ritual victims, and they were not always scrupulous about political allegiances when laying ambushes in accessible villages (Williams 1931:505–506; Jaggar *Ms.:* Diary, April 27, 1842; Cross *Ms.:* Diary, Feb. 1, 1839; Hocart, *HF:* re Rewa; Lyth *Ms.:* Journal, Feb. 23, 1854, Mar. 9, 1854; Thomson 1968[1908]:35).[11]

---

[11] It was also possible that a war party would turn upon an in-married man from another "land" (*vanua*) when frustrated in the attempt to procure *bakola* (e.g. Lyth *Ms.,* Journal, Oct. 21, 1853).

Statistical judgments of the extent of cannibalism have not yet been formulated. In connection with the wars waged in the earlier 19th century by Bau, Rewa, Cakaudrove, and other major chiefdoms, cannibalism was frequent and sometimes orgiastic (cf. Derrick 1950; Tippett 1973). Reverend Hunt estimated that during a five-year period in the 1840s, not fewer than 500 people had been eaten within 15 miles of his residence at Viwa, neighbor-island to Bau (in Lyth *Ms.:* Notebook, B552).[12] Massacres of more than 300 people were known to follow the sacking of large towns, as when Rewa was stormed by Bau in December 1845. On such occasions, more *bakola* were available than could be consumed (e.g., Lyth *Ms.:* Journal, Sept. 13, 1847; *Ms.:* Reminiscences, re Lokia massacre, B548). The notorious chief Ra Udreudre of Rakiraki made an alignment of stones, one for each victim, in testimony to his cannibal exploits; Reverend Lyth, shown the stones by the chief's son, counted 872 (*Ms.:* Voyaging Journal 1, Nov. 21, 1848).

The victims, or at least certain selected corpses among the enemy dead, were subject to multiple sacrifice: first by the slayer who, shouting his lineage (*mataqali* or *yavusa*) war cry, dedicated the body on the field of battle to his own god; then by the ruling chief and/or the priest at the major temple of the land. At Bau and other places, this prestation to the god of the land entailed a second killing; the head of the victim was dashed against a stone in the temple precincts, thus according the brains to the god. (Lyth, Hunt, Williams, Cross, Jaggar and Calvert provide numerous descriptions of the sacrifices in their papers.) Men, women and children were all eaten, but apart from the general rule that bodies were cooked overnight in underground ovens to be consumed the following day, and that a priest presided over the preparations, the culinary treatment of the corpse varied regionally, as well as by the number and status of the slain and according to the military or ritual occasion. Gau Islanders were famous for cooking bodies whole (Lyth *Ms.:* Missionary Pocket Book; cf. Hunt to Worth, copied in Lyth *Ms.:* Notebook, B552). A widespread procedure was to take three joints from

---

[12] Taking the year 1843 and the first half of 1844, cannibal feasts are noted for the following dates in R. B. Lyth's Journal at Somosomo (numbers of victims in parenthesis): Feb. 22, 1843 (8 or 9); May 28, 1843 (1); June 10, 1843 (near 50); July 5, 1843 (13); Sept. 23, 1843 (1); Jan. 28, 1844 (1); Feb. 2, 1844 (3); Feb. 22, 1844 (1); May 27, 1844 (1).

each limb, in the following sequence: right hand, left foot, left hand right foot, right forearm, left lower leg, and so forth (cf. Calvert *Ms.:* Vewa Record, Aug. 5, 1853). Reverend Lyth, who was a physician, provides a meticulous anatomical description of a dissection, in preparation for the oven, to which he was an eyewitness (*Ms.:* Journal, Sept. 14, 1840).

Consecrated to the god, the *bakola* assumed a divine status. Like a high chief's own body, all parts of the corpse had ritual terms of reference (Thomson 1968[1908]:104-105). Contact with the cooked flesh had to be mediated: a special "cannibal fork" was used in eating—just as those who held aloft the newborn royal infant or prepared the corpse of a deceased chief could not directly feed themselves; or conversely, the high chief, as divine, could not touch cooked food but was fed by others. The extent of the distribution of *bakola* again varied according to the number slain and the occasion. The ranking chief (Roko Tui), priests and other land chieftains took priority; but if the supply were sufficient, pieces of the cooked victims were distributed to all the mature and young men, and even to women and children. (Thus sometimes it is said that the Roko Tui is the sole cannibal, as at Bau, but the statement is a typical Fijian expression of a diacritic priority in the form of a privative contrast; it should not be taken as an empirical observation or generalization—cf. Waterhouse 1866:242.) *Bakola,* raw or cooked, might also be sent to certain allied warriors (*bati*) of other lands, and to high chiefs elsewhere with whom the local paramount had special relationships. The heart, tongue, and liver of the *bakola*—as well as legs, arms, loins, and shoulders—are variously mentioned as chiefly parts, the hands and feet as the portions of low-ranking warriors or young men (*caura vou*). From the gourmet point of view, the informants of the Methodist missionaries generally agreed that the breasts of young women made the choicest repast. (On these matters of distribution and consumption, apart from the missionary records, see, among others; Clunie 1977; Lockerby et al. 1925; Thomson 1968[1908]; Seeman 1973[1862]; Diapea 1928; Jackson (alias Diapea) in Erskine 1967[1853]; Wallis 1851; Endicott 1923; Williams 1859; Williams 1931.)

To return to the argument, we have seen that the stranger-king undertakes to supply cooked men to the land in return for the raw women originally ceded him by the indigenous people. Lévi-Strauss did not invent these terms of exchange. Fijians themselves make the association. Hocart recounts the apology of the Lau chief to the master-builder of his sacred canoe: that the chief was regrettably unable to give in return the bodies of young men or else a woman "brought raw" *(kau droka mai)*; for Christianity, he explained, "spoils our feasts" (Hocart 1929:129). The equation is possible because in the global system of sacrifice, raw women and cooked men have the same finality. Both are reproductive, "life-giving": the woman directly, the sacrificial victim as means of the exchange of *mana* between men and gods. Here, then, is another expression of their equivalence: a barren wife is not strangled to accompany the soul of her husband to the afterworld *(Bulu)*, ancestral source of human and natural reproduction; and as for the deceased warrior who had never killed, never brought home a human sacrifice, he is condemned to endlessly pound a pile of shit with his warclub, through all eternity (Fison 1904:xx).[13]

Indeed, the developed Fijian chiefdom is organized by an elaborate cycle of exchange of raw women for cooked men between a basic trio of social cum cosmic categories: foreign warriors, immigrant chiefs, and indigenous members of the land. Space permits me to speak of the essentials only. The elementary synthesis of the stranger-king and the native people, synthesis that domesticates the immigrant cannibal, thereby motivates the appearance in the polity of a third term: the "dangerous men" *(tamata rerevaki)*, foreign warriors and assassins whose function is the procurement of human sacrificial victims from beyond the land. Some of these warriors are "sea people" *(kai wai)*, including turtle-fishers who are also, as Fijians say, fishers of men.[14] Some are land allies or *bati (balavu)*, a term that means "border" and "tooth (that bites the victim)" as well as "warrior." The several foreign allies are originally attached to the

---

[13] It is, as the Maori say, "the battlefield with man; childbirth with woman" (Firth 1926: 263-264). The Aztec formed and acted on the same representation of social reproduction.

[14] The Lasakau fishers of Bau were the most famous "dangerous men," not merely in war but because when sent by the chief for ritual victims, their methods were terrifying: "The Lasakauans are distinguished by their cruel way of butchering [i.e., killing, not carving for the oven] their enemies. It is their usual plan to take their victims alive, if possible, and then after a course of cruel suspense and often diabolical mockery and torture, to put them to death" (Lyth *Ms.*: Journal, July 30, 1847). They also developed a reputation for cunning and duplicity in attack, and indifference as to possible relationships of common descent to their victims (Hocart 1952:54-55; Calvert *Ms.*: Vewa Record, July 26, 1853).

chief and chiefdom by the gift of a royal daughter. They are wife-takers to the chiefly line, as the chiefs are wife-takers to the indigenous people. And as the chief shares bodies with the people in return for the woman, so do the foreign warriors bring bodies to him.[15]

As I speak only of essentials, I can merely mention the transformations of men and women, raw and cooked, through the cycle that preserve the distinctions between categories and their hierarchical arrangement. In the birth rituals of the royal child, both the mother—the raw women the chief had obtained from the native people—and her child are symbolically cooked. If this enculturates them, incorporates them from the natural-spiritual world (Lévi-Strauss 1970:335-336), it also means the daughter passed on by the chief to his foreign killers is first reduced to human status: an important aspect of the relative neutralization of the status of the foreign warrior as uterine nephew to the chiefly line. In exchange for the cooked daughter, the warrior-allies provide the chief with raw men. These *bakola* are identified with (or, in the case of failure to take a victim, even interchangeable with) their killers. But the offerings are again cooked and reduced in spiritual value before they are shared with the indigenous cultivators, whose initial surrender of the raw woman had initiated the entire cycle. The transformations between raw and cooked thus sustain the hierarchical as well as the mediate position of the chief, above and between his land people and his sea people, his cultivators and his fishers, his domestic subjects and his foreign allies, his internal guardians and his external assassins. It is an organization of all of nature as well as all society, and of production as well as polity, of which nothing more is said here, except how the chief got into position to constitute it. The chief must die as a victim before he is reborn as the god.

By a symbolic death at the hands of the people—which, history shows, may prove to have been a dress rehearsal—the immigrant chief is domesticated, transmuted thus from foreign cannibal to

---

[15] The triadic structure of the Fijian chiefdom is discussed in a little more detail in Sahlins (1981). Here also it is noted that the flow of women against (cooked) men is specifically a *founding transaction*, establishing the perpetual relationship between lines; it is not necessarily—and certainly not prescriptively—continued as an empirical system of generalized exchange.

divine benefactor. We thus return to the myth of Tabua. In an appended note, the recorder (Heffernan?) calls attention to the Fijian custom of eating the crews of shipwrecked canoes, "people with salt water in their eyes." The myth posits the origin of this custom as the origin of cannibalism in general.[16] But it is critical for interpretation that the consumption of castaways is not a mere sequitur to the events of the story. For Fijian auditors, the custom is a *presupposition* that gives the sense of these events. Tabua should have been eaten straight away. The myth thus consists of successive attempts of the hero to provide a substitute for himself as food, finding in the end a form that completes the transaction as bridewealth. The first attempt was unsuccessful. Instead of his own body, Tabua offers his prospective father-in-law ordinary vegetable food. But cultivated crops are just that, ordinary food, whereas the *bakola* is the marked form of food and the occasion of extraordinary feasts. In the second and successful attempt, the hero mediates the discrepancy between common food and a cooked man by presenting a more mediated mode of himself as whale teeth (*tabua*). Again the Fijian audience would immediately seize the equivalence, Tabua being the man's own name. But the myth takes the trouble to establish the identity, both metaphorically and metonymically, by means of events. Metaphorically, the whale is analogous to the man in that both are victims of an accident at sea who drift ashore at the same time. Metonymically, the man loses his own teeth in the act of extracting the whale's teeth, which is also an inverted metonym of Tabua's status as cannibal victim, entailing the substitution of that by which he bites food for himself as food. Hence the deceit by which the hero avoids his own death and obtains the women is also a true sacrifice, he having given part of himself for these greater benefits.

The burden of our tale can now be summarized. Presented by the arrival of a dangerous cannibal with an acute form of the Tylorian

---

[16] The assertion of an identity between cannibalism in general and the consumption of shipwrecked persons may in fact be logically adequate, given Fijian custom. Close descriptions by, or taken from, eyewitnesses indicate that in maritime Fiji the enemy dead destined for sacrifice were cut adrift from the victorious canoes and allowed to float ashore, rather than carried to land (MMS-SOAS: In-Letters: Hazelwood to General Secretaries, Oct. 22, 1847; Cargill 1977:158; Gordon Cumming 1886:119). Similarly at Rewa, Jaggar speaks of victims being floated or dragged through the river to shore (Journal, Sept. 5, 1840). The saying goes that "castaways are sent by the gods to feast the chiefs" (Pritchard 1968[1866]). Conversely, all cannibal victims may have been castaways.

alternative between marrying out or dying out, the Fijians were able to invent a solution that would satisfy all appetites by marrying out and dining out. An initial opposition of antisocial and antagonistic elements is transformed into the relationships of a human society, a process the myth allows us to conceive alternately as an effect of the exchange of women or as an exchange effected by them. But the transformation also entails sublimation. The reproductive powers gained by Tabua are matched by the losses of his indigenous father-in-law, who is not only deprived of his daughters but of his beard, a particular sign of virility affected by the aging chief whose craft is ebbing. Thus the origin of the incest tabu and exogamy, and of another transaction also indispensable to society. If the old man loses his beard, the *quondam* cannibal loses his teeth. Hereafter, the immigrant chief forgoes eating the land, or consumes it rather in the benign form of marrying the daughters; and instead of being eaten by the native people, he agrees to feed them on men who are, like himself, castaways from beyond. The chief will give feast to the people on bodies of his own kind.

At the conclusion of the Bau installation ceremonies, the paramount chief (*Vunivalu*) rewards the native owner who invested him with cannibal victims taken by his foreign fishers (Hocart 1929:70). The gift is the Fijian sequitur to a general feature of the divine king's coronation, on which Hocart (1969a) has said much. The king dies, to be reborn as a domesticated god. In Fijian rites of this type, the moment of the king's death is precisely the moment of his accession, when he drinks the sacred kava of the land. But kava is a poison. Variants of the Tongan and Rotuman tale of its origins are widely told in Fiji (Bott 1972; Leach 1972). By the Lau version, kava grew from the leprous body of a child of the native people who had at first been killed for the chief's feast but was buried instead.[17] Kava is thus brought to the Lau installation by a land chieftain, who proceeds to dismember the root by the violent thrusts of a sharp-pointed stick (traditionally a spear?). Having taken the sacred cup, the chief is in the state of intoxication Fijians know as "dead from" (*mateni*) or "dead from kava" (*mate ni yaqona*), to recover from which is specifically "to live" (*bula*). The ruler is immediately revived by a

---

[17] On the problem of the sex of the sacrificial child in the Lau myth, see Sahlins (1981), where a few further details and bibliographic notices of the Lau installations are also found.

cup of fresh water, exclusive privilege of the chief and distinctive feature of his installation. But he is now in a transformed state, and the succeeding ceremonies imitate those of a noble birth. After the purification appropriate to these rites, the chief is carried again to the center of the village, guarded by warriors from the most indigenous stock of the land, who are singing a song of victory. Is it the victory of the newly crowned king? The song these warriors sing as the chief passes between their lines is the same they intone over the body of a cannibal victim.

Domesticated ritually, the sacred Fijian chief appears historically as the provider of the cannibal feast, but in the ambiguous double sense of feeder of the people and their food. Taken in war from beyond the land, in the privileged case, from great enemies and rival chiefs, the cannibal victims are in effect of the nature of the ruling chief himself—terrible outside gods. This helps explain certain 19th-century reports of the ambivalent treatment accorded the corpses of the most honored or most hated enemies, including parodies of the installation kava rites (Endicott 1923:59–60; Fowler 1845). Hence also the beautiful chant published by Thomas Williams (1859:163), wherein the *bakola* is made to say, as he is dragged to the place of sacrifice by triumphant warriors and mocking women:

Yari au malua,	Drag me gently,
Yari au malua,	Drag me gently,
Koi au na saro ni	I am the champion of
nomu vanua.	your land.

CONCLUSION

By a kind of dialogue between myth and practice, I have tried to explicate the cultural sense of cannibalism in traditional Fiji. Plainly, the intent was to shift the discussion away from current debates about the purported nonexistence of cannibalism or its supposed nutritional virtues. Since cannibalism in an institutional form, particularly exo-cannibalism, is normally an aspect of sacrifice, and concerned with the symbolic values of certain parts only of certain selected victims, something is to be said for definitions of the practice that would make it widespread, tolerating even figurative expressions as permutations of a more general common principle. To the contrary, it would be difficult to agree with the Christian missionary, who on partaking the Lord's Supper with a small group of Marquesan converts, thought he was witness to a remarkable religious change, since only a few years before these inveterate cannibals had been eating the flesh of their fellow men: "All had eaten human flesh, and drunk the blood of their enemies. They were now sitting at the feet of Jesus, and in their right minds, eating and drinking the emblems of that body which was broken, and that blood which was shed for man" (Coan 1882:173). The problem, of course, is that cannibalism is always "symbolic," even when it is "real."

As for origins, logic would also suggest we start from the sacrificial finalities. It could even be claimed that cannibalism exists *in nuce* in most sacrifice, inasmuch as the victim must be identified with the sacrifier and is often consumed: either by the congregation as communion or by the sacrificer (priest) as representative of the god.[18] On the other hand, all other purposes cannibalism may serve, such as functional rationale for military conquest, are logically unable to specify the practice and thus appear as secondary formations. Political aggression is indeed logically demanded by human sacrifice, but human sacrifice is not required for political aggression. In any event, discussion of such issues seems preferable to the dilemma posed by current theories, which offer us the alternative of debating the existence of a cannibalism we have not understood, or not understanding the existence of the cannibalism we are debating.

The cultural sense of cannibalism is the concept of it as set by its place in a total cultural scheme, which gives it a differential value in relationship to other categories or concepts. So the Fijian *bakola* or "cannibal victim" is determined as a meaning by its relationships to chiefs, gods, turtles, whale teeth, and women. This meaning (or set of meanings) is an expression of the conceptual order in customs

---

[18] "La valeur relative de chaque victime est déterminée par le degré d'identification qui existe entre elle et le sacrifiant: cette hiérarchie détermine donc jusqu'à quel point on donne soi-même. De ce point de vue, le sacrifice humain n'est pas une catégorie a part, mais la révélation de l'essence de tout sacrifice" (Valeri, in press). So the theory of Waterhouse (1866:312) on Fijian cannibalism: "One tradition notices that the human body was at first offered to the gods, in consideration of its being the best sacrifice that could be found." Cannibalism thus arose, Waterhouse speculates, by analogy to offerings of food, which are afterwards consumed.

themselves, being objectified precisely to the extent it is intersub-jective. It ought not be reduced, then, to the value of *bakola* to the acting subjects, who variously take consciousness of the cultural sense as an interest or intentional value, according to their respec-tive social experiences. For over 200 years now, the Europeans best acquainted with Fijians have been trying to find out what moved them to eat each other. But as precisely as they have been seeking the reason in the practice from the various reasons people may have for practicing it, so the "explanations" proposed have been generally true, mutually contradictory, and universally insufficient.

Apart from a presumed shortage of other meat — an idea already discarded by Captain Cook (1967:164) and repeatably disproved since — virtually all the other reasons asserted for Fijian cannibalism have been empirically supportable, often by the direct statements of famous cannibals. Revenge, a gourmet appreciation of human flesh, political ambition, masculine bravado, fear of the chief or because it is custom: all these and similar motives have been well and truly marked. For all are obviously complementary to the cultural sense of cannibalism. Yet all of them put together cannot logically motivate the meaningful content of a custom which, as constituted by relationships to other customs, is the condition of their own possibility as appropriate motives.[19]

---

[19] Excellent statements on their own motives by reformed cannibals are found in Lyth's papers, especially in B548, "Reminiscences." One of note by a certain Samani, now Christian and formerly "a great cannibal," reads (in Lyth's transcription): "e tawa kania ko'iau m'u sa vinakata; e na qaciqacia ga kei na viavia levu" ("I didn't eat [human flesh] because I liked it; it was from pride only and ambition.") Hunt's journals and papers (*Ms.*) offer, at different times, different reasons. Early on (Hunt to General Secretaries, June 29, 1839), he thought that political motives were as important as religious ones, but the only answer he ever got to direct inquiry was "custom." By 1842 (Letter to "Dear Friend," September 17, 1842), Hunt was assured that "they have abundance of provisions, so that cannibalism is never necessary." And in 1848, in a memorandum to Captain Worth of H.M.S. *Calypso*, he concludes that "it is quite a mistake to suppose they eat human flesh merely for revenge. Many of them have only one reason namely, because they prefer it to other food. Others eat it from pride, others no doubt in time of War from Revenge" (copy in Lyth *Ms.*, Notebook [B552]; cf. Waterhouse 1866:312). Seemann's experiences in this regard are revealing:

But as a general rule *bokola* was not regarded in the shape of food; and when some of the chiefs told foreigners, who again and again would attack them about a custom intimately connected with the whole fabric of their society, and not to be abolished by a single resolution, that they in-dulged in eating it because their country furnished nothing but pork, being destitute of beef and all other kinds of meat, they simply wished to offer some excuse which might satisfy their in-quisitors for the moment. [Seeman 1973(1862):181]

I do not mean to deny the historic role of interest and action, but only to point out that its form and effects are contingent on the existing cultural order. We will not be able to read the contents of customs by short-circuiting this order and starting instead with their values to individual subjects. Still less would Fijian cannibalism be deducible from an abstract-collective subject, "the population" with its biological "needs," figured thus organically and independently of its mode of cultural organization. By comparison, then, with all the eternal verities, from the utilitarian to the Freudian, the cultural sense of cannibalism is the true beginning of a historical wisdom. For the cultural sense, like the distinctive practices it organizes, has the virtue of being arbitrary *and* logical, having meanings peculiar to the group yet intelligible to the species. Practices objectively remote from ourselves can thus be made subjectively familiar. Knowing the cultural logic, we are uniquely able to comprehend the specific characteristics of cannibal custom as predicates of more general principles. Even from the sketchy observations on Fijian cannibalism presented here, we can begin to grasp the reason in a thousand correlated customs I have not had time to mention: why a reputation for cruelty and cannibalistic excess is a qualification for the chiefship among contending heirs; why excited chiefs have been known to eat parts of the victim raw or underdone; why the ceremonies and transactions of cannibalism are the same as those of turtle-fishing; why the manslayer is celebrated as a "short (-time) chief" (*turaga lekaleka*), while his club—the "penis of the warrior"—is destined to be enshrined in a sacred place as the "ancestral friend" of his descendants; or why his advent is greeted by wild scenes of sexual license, even as morsels of the cooked victim are pressed against the lips of sucking babes, and the raw genitals are hung upon the sacred tree, shrine of the god.

The inner sense of cannibalism is the logic, also, in its known development. European trade and the beginnings of colonial settlement in the earlier 19th century fueled the ovens of cannibalism in Fiji to the point of incandescence. According to respectable observers, the traffic in whale teeth was decisive to this development (Toganivalu *Ms.;* Quain 1948:21-22; cf. Pritchard 1968[1866]: 332). Yet, from the European side nothing about the trade was unique: the same products were demanded as elsewhere in the Pacific, often by the same traders practicing the same methods. If the Fijian reaction was distinctively an intensification of transactions in whale teeth and cannibalism, this effect clearly was orchestrated by the culture in place. Capitalism may be a system of bigger fish eating smaller fish, but not everywhere was the competitive ideal so literally assimilated as a consuming passion. If I have begun with myth to finish with history, it is because, as I have tried to show, the historical practice of cannibalism can alternately serve as the concrete referent of a mythical theory or its behavioral metaphor.

REFERENCES

Note on Abbreviations
ML   Mitchell Library, Library of New South Wales, Sydney.
MMS-SOAS   Papers of the Methodist Missionary Society, deposited at the Library, School of Oriental and African Studies, University of London.

BOTT, ELIZABETH.   1972   Psychoanalysis and Ceremony *and* A Rejoinder to Edmund Leach. *The Interpretation of Ritual,* (J. S. La Fontaine, ed.) pp. 205-237; 277-282. London: Tavistock.
BREWSTER, A. M.   *Ms.*   The Chronicles of the Noikoro Tribe, National Archives of Fiji (CS2195 FS B2).
CALVERT, REVEREND JAMES.   *Ms.*   Papers of James Calvert, MMS-SOAS.
CARGILL, REVEREND DAVID.   1977.   *The Diaries and Correspondence of David Cargill, 1832-1843.* (Albert J. Schutz, ed.). Canberra: The Australian National University Press.
CLUNIE, FERGUS.   1977.   *Fijian Weapons and Warfare.* Bulletin of the Fiji Museum No. 2. Suva: Fiji Times and Herald.
COAN, TITUS.   1882.   *Life in Hawaii: An Autobiographic Sketch of Mission Life and Labors (1835-1881).* New York: Randolph.
COOK, JAMES.   1967.   *The Journals of Captain James Cook: III. The Voyage of the Resolution and Discovery, 1776-1780.* (J. C. Beaglehole, ed.). Cambridge: Hakluyt Society, Cambridge University Press.
CROSS, REVEREND WILLIAM.   *Ms.*   Diary of Reverend William Cross. ML (MOM336).
DERRICK, R. A.   1950.   *A History of Fiji.* (Revised ed.). Suva: Government Press.
DIAPEA, WILLIAM.   1928.   *Cannibal Jack: The True Autobiography of a White Man In the South Seas.* London: Faber and Gwyer.
DURKHEIM, EMILE.   1947.   *The Elementary Forms of Religious Life.* New York: Free Press of Glencoe.
ENDICOTT, W.   1923.   *Wrecked among Cannibals in the Fijis.* Salem: Marine Research Society.
ERSKINE, JOHN ELPHINSTON.   1967[1853].   *Journal of a Cruise among the Islands of the Western Pacific.* London: Dawsons of Pall Mall.
FIRTH, RAYMOND.   1926.   Proverbs in Native Life with Special Reference to Those of the Maori. *Folklore* 37:134-153, 245-270.
FISON, LORIMER.   1904.   *Tales from Old Fiji.* London: Moring.

FOWLER, HENRY. 1845. Description of a Cannibal Feast at the Feejee Islands. *Danvers Courier,* August 16, 1845. Microfilm Copy, Pacific Manuscripts Bureau Doc 299, Microfilm Reel 225, University of Hawaii Library.

GORDON, SIR ARTHUR. *Ms.* Stanmore Collection. Cambridge University, Museum of Archaeology and Anthropology.

GORDON CUMMING, C. F. 1882. *At Home in Fiji.* Edinburgh and London: Blackwood and Sons.

HANDY, E. S. CRAIGHILL and MARY KAWENA PUKUI. 1972. *The Polynesian Family System in Ka-'u, Hawai'i.* Rutland (Vt.) and Tokyo: Charles E. Tuttle.

HEUSCH, LUC DE. (et al.) 1962. *Le pouvoir et le sacré.* Annales du Centre d'Etude des Religions 1. Brussels; Universite Libre de Bruxelles.

HOCART, A. M. *FN.* Fijian field notes. Microfilm in University of Chicago Libraries of manuscript original in the Turnbull Library, Wellington, N.Z.

————. *HF.* The Heart of Fiji. Microfilm in University of Chicago Libraries of manuscript original in Turnbull Library, Wellington, N.Z.

————. 1912. On the Meaning of Kalou and the Origin of Fijian Temples. *Journal of the Royal Anthropological Institute* 42:437–449.

————. 1915. Chieftainship and the Sister's Son in the Pacific. *American Anthropologist* 17:631–646.

————. 1929. *The Lau Islands, Fiji.* Bernice P. Bishop Museum Bulletin 62. Honolulu: Bishop Museum Press.

————. 1952. *The Northern States of Fiji.* Royal Anthropological Institute of Great Britain and Ireland, Occasional Publication 11. London: The Institute.

————. 1969a[1927]. *Kingship.* Oxford, Eng.: Oxford University Press.

————. 1969b[1952]. *The Life-Giving Myth.* London: Tavistock.

————. 1970[1936]. *Kings and Councillors.* Chicago: University of Chicago Press.

HUNT, REVEREND JOHN. *Ms.* Journals and Papers of Rev. John Hunt. MMS-SOAS.

JAGGAR, REVEREND THOMAS JAMES. *Ms.* Diaries of Thomas James Jaggar, 1837-1843. Microfilm in Pacific Collection, Adelaide University Library of original in National Archives of Fiji.

LEACH, EDMUND. 1972. The Structure of Symbolism *and* Appendix. *The Interpretation of Ritual* (J. S. La Fontaine, ed.), pp. 239-275, 283-284. London: Tavistock.

LÉVI-STRAUSS, CLAUDE. 1970. *The Raw and the Cooked.* New York and Evanston: Harper Torchbooks.

LOCKERBY, WILLIAM (et al.). 1925. *The Journal of William Lockerby* (Sir Everard Imthurn and Leonard C. Wharton, eds.). London: Hakluyt Society. (Contains also papers of Samuel Patterson, L.M.S. Missionaries, etc.)

LYTH, REVEREND RICHARD BURDSALL. *Ms.* Papers and Journals of Reverend Richard Burdsall Lyth. ML.

MMS-SOAS. In-Letters: To the Methodist Missionary Society, London, 1835-1857.

PRITCHARD, W. T. 1968[1866]. *Polynesian Reminiscences.* London: Dawsons of Pall Mall.

QUAIN, BUELL. 1948. *Fijian Village.* Chicago: University of Chicago Press.

RABUKA, NIKO. 1911. Ai sau ni taro ni ka me kilai. *Na Mata,* Nos. 250-251.

REID, A. C. 1977. The Fruit of the Rewa: Oral Traditions and the Growth of the Pre-Christian Lakeba State. *Journal of Pacific History* 12:2-24.

ROKOWAQA, EPELI. n.d.   *Ai Tukutuku kei Viti.* Suva: no publisher. (A copy of this rare book is available in the National Archives of Fiji.)

SAHLINS, MARSHALL. 1981. The Stranger-King, or Dumézil among the Fijians. *Journal of Pacific History.* 16:107–132.

SEEMAN, BERTHOLD. 1973[1862]. *Viti: an Account of a Government Mission to the Vitian or Fijian Islands 1860–1861.* London: Dawsons of Pall Mall.

THOMPSON, LAURA. 1940. *Southern Lau, Fiji: An Ethnography.* Bernice P. Bishop Museum Bulletin 232. Honolulu: Bishop Museum Press.

THOMSON, BASIL. 1968[1908]. *The Fijians: A Study of the Decay of Custom.* London: Dawsons of Pall Mall.

TIPPETT, A. R. 1973. *Aspects of Pacific Ethno-history.* Pasadena: William Carey Library.

TOGANIVALU, RATU DEVE. Ms. *Ai Tukutuku kei BAu.* National Archives of Fiji (F62/247).

————. 1918. Fijian Property and Gear. *Transactions of the Fijian Society,* pp. 1–18.

VALERI, VALERIO. In press. *Hai Kanaka: The Hawaiian Chief and his Sacrifice.* Chicago: University of Chicago Press.

WALLIS, MARY DAVID COOK ("A Lady"). 1851. *Life in Feejee, or, Five Years among the Cannibals.* Boston: Heath.

WATERHOUSE, REVEREND JOSEPH. 1866. *The King and People of Fiji.* London: Wesleyan Conference Office.

WHITE, JOHN. 1887–1890. *Ancient History of the Maori.* 6 vols. Wellington: Government Printer.

WILKES, CHARLES. 1845. *Narrative of the United States Exploring Expedition during the Years 1838, 1839, 1840, 1841, 1842.* 5 vols. Philadelphia: Lea and Blanchard.

WILLIAMS, REVEREND THOMAS. 1931. *The Journal of Thomas Williams; Missionary in Fiji, 1840–1853.* 2 vols. (G. C. Henderson, ed.). Sydney: Angus and Robertson.

WILLIAMS, THOMAS, and JAMES CALVERT. 1859. *Fiji and the Fijians.* New York: Appleton.

Cannibalism

Symbolic Production and Consumption

SHIRLEY LINDENBAUM

In his discussion of the American Anthropological Association-published symposium on male-female relations in New Guinea, Langness (1976) observes that those who were yesterday social anthropologists and cultural ecologists have become, almost without warning, symbolic anthropologists of varying kinds. Pointing to four recognizable schools of symbolic analysis, he notes that many of the papers in the symposium seem to belong to more than one of these "traditions," although their affiliation is never made clear. He suggests that the epistemological and methodological status of symbolic anthropology depends on acknowledging pioneers and contemporaries in the field and he calls particularly for recognition of the common ground shared by symbolic anthropology and psychology.

The papers in the present collection illustrate the eclecticism that now characterizes the symbolic approach — an expanded perspective that includes the psychological dimension proposed by Langness. Not surprisingly, such augmentation entails some amount of disciplinary untidiness. The various styles of analysis displayed in these essays read like a list of the actors' accomplishments enumerated at the court of the King of Denmark: cognitive, semiotic,

SHIRLEY LINDENBAUM is Associate Professor of Anthropology at the New School for Social Research.

I would like to thank Jane Schneider and Pam Smith for their critical reading of an earlier draft of this paper.

94

philosophical, psychoanalytic, cultural, French-structuralist, British-structuralist, structural-historical, and structural-functional-historical, all unified by a common concern to explore the belief systems and cultural constructions that underlie behavior. A thoroughgoing materialist approach, the focus of much recent attention in the literature on cannibalism (Harris 1977; Harner 1977; Dornstreich and Morren 1974), is notably absent from the collection presented here.

This mixing of methods may be an unavoidable current trend, for when speaking of the French structuralist enterprise, Lévi-Strauss noted recently that his generation had been concerned with introducing a bit of rigor into the discipline and had consequently tried to limit the number of variables to be considered. The next generation was thus in a position to broaden its range (Lévi-Strauss, Godelier, and Auge 1976). Moreover, if the problem facing symbolic analysis in the early 1970s was the self-conscious emergence of a symbolic anthropology capable of acknowledging its common ground with psychology,[1] the present predicament concerns the relationship of symbolic anthropology to historical processes, a matter I explore more fully below.

The strength of symbolic analysis lies in the facility with which it encompasses different kinds of phenomena and reveals connections that would otherwise remain implicit or hidden. Thus, in the papers we have here, cannibalism emerges less as a single form of behavior located in a number of out-of-the-way places, than as an activity to be comprehended by reference to its place in particular cultural orbits. Sahlins, for instance, discloses a system of relationships among persons and objects such that the meaning of Fijian cannibalism is seen to derive from its relationship to chiefs, gods, turtles, whale teeth, and women. Tuzin explores an image of cannibalism relevant to Arapesh psychic integrity and cultural identity and to other points in the Arapesh metaphysical scheme. Poole points to the interdependencies to be traced between different modes of anthropophagy and the Bimin-Kuskusmin partition of their known universe into four concentric zones of being, a projection inward on

---

[1] In a recent essay, Lewis (1977) notes that British social anthropologists, despite their rejection of it, have been closet psychologists all along.

gender and self as well as outward on a wider ethnic landscape. Gillison's exploration of the symbolic parallels between representations of Gimi cannibalism and the mythic theft from women of sacred bamboo flutes reveals the connections that exist between beliefs about reincarnation and the cultural assignment of the role of cannibalism to Gimi women. By considering Sherbro categorical anomalies, MacCormack explicates the political meanings projected by the vigorous, strong, and fecund duiker and hippopotamus with their human counterparts, the Poro, Sande, and Thoma societies on the one hand, and the willful, destructive, consuming leopard and crocodile with their human counterparts, the cannibal societies of the Leopard and Alligator on the other. Accusations of cannibalism emerge as a recurrent idiom of Sherbro political theatre.

The position of all of the papers, clearly enunciated by several authors, is that an adequate anthropological analysis goes beyond the matter of whether or not cannibalism actually occurs, and requires an investigation of the symbolic or ideological dimensions of reported acts or beliefs (see Poole, this volume). Thus, we are confronted with the double, or perhaps simultaneous, tasks of eliciting for each culture a coherent "world view" as well as evaluating those beliefs and representations together with what we observe to be the social behaviors and social realities. This is not a matter of simple translation, but in fact poses a current methodological conundrum, resolved in a variety of ways by anthropologists with different forebears. The basic issue is "whether symbols reflect, express, or otherwise correspond to social arrangements, or on the other hand, act so as to mask, obfuscate, or deny social realities," especially structures of inequality (Silverman 1981:163–164).[2] Alternatively, does social life consist of practical knowledge and ritual cognition, the one a system by which we know the world, and the other the system by which we hide it (Bloch 1977; Bourdillon 1978)?

Sahlins's approach to the problem here raises analytic sophistication to another level. By entering into a double structuralist

---

[2] See also Ortner and Whitehead (1981) where the distinction is drawn between the Durkheimian view of cultural features as "reflections" of social structures, and the Marxist position that culture is an ideological distortion of social reality, "mystifying" the sources of oppression and exploitation. Weber, by way of Parsons and Geertz, is presented here as the mediator, turning analytic attention to the meanings of actor-mediated symbols.

discourse of sorts, he shows how outsiders interacted with and interpreted their encounters with indigenous people of the land, how the indigenous Fijians reciprocally interacted with and interpreted their encounters with outsiders, and the way both were mutually transformed in the process. As a matter of style, the ethnographic and historical information is separated from the general and structural account, but the paper's final resting place is that myth, ritual, and historic action give meaning each to the other. Actions and their effects take their form from existing cultural orders. By a kind of elision, historical practice is said to be both a concrete referent of mythic thought and its behavioral metaphor. This last twist conveys Sahlins's unique dialectic vision, a view that does away with the so-called myth/reality problem. By conveying the filaments of connection among persons, things, and events, attention is drawn to the simultaneity of meaning in apparently disparate transactions. The strength of the method lies in the revelation of systemic and transforming cultural logics, although much of its persuasive power stems from the elegance of Sahlins's execution. With this approach, the way in which symbols reflect and/or mask social reality is not considered problematic. The manner in which the other authors confront this issue is discussed later.

The explicit attempt to incorporate historical processes into the analysis, however, allows for the consideration of new problems, and also casts an intensified light on older ways of viewing things. Many of the papers show the enlivening effect of this historical sense. Tuzin's sensitive reflections upon the Arapesh refusal to think that the Japanese had stooped to cannibalism from hunger shows us a culturally constituted intellectual and philosophical system at a moment of poignant vulnerability. To admit that this might have occurred would be to dismantle a key support upon which Arapesh cultural identity depended. Perhaps the sense of change might be pushed even further to view the emotional potency of the Arapesh reaction to the idea as going beyond the recognition that the Japanese had become their "fathers." In many ways, related to the nightmare itself, the Arapesh world seems to be falling apart. The mythic and ritual fantasy of parents devouring their children appears to be creeping closer to home, for cult spirits are now said to have "begun feasting in earnest on their own people," and many routine deaths in the village are now colored with cannibalistic overtones. The final unthinkable step in this cultural debacle perhaps lies in the loss of authority by senior over junior men, seniors no longer able to sustain or increase the ritual sanctions that keep transgressing juniors in line. These disciplinary boundaries, maintained until recently by the accepted charade that the Tambaran spirit of the seniors "eats the food" levied on defaulting juniors (an image of hierarchical devouring), are now blurred by new powers and opportunities available to young men (Tuzin 1976:292). The intensity of response to the notion of parental cannibalism thus occurs in the context of a heightened sense of the fragility of lines of authority, suggested in the not-to-be-admitted notion that the deranged cannibals, the deculturated beings, could well be themselves.

A historical sense is also important to MacCormack's perceptive account of the son who killed the cannibalistic crocodiles of his father's group, but who remained ambivalent about killing the "mana" of his father, another account of the conflicting interests of generations in changing times. It is noticeable too that Sherbro notions of cannibalism have a postcolonial ring to them. The first reported spate of cannibal accusations takes place in the context of appeals to government authorities for whom this was a preordained category of moral default. Seen historically, Sherbro cannibal accusations thus take shape as much from the changing interactions of Sherbro with outsiders as from the imagery spawned by local culture.

Poole's ethnographically refined account of Bimin-Kuskusmin beliefs and practices, particularly those in which they capture and ritually consume certain parts of their current major enemies, the Oksapmin, may also be seen in the light of a historically relevant reversal of dominance in the trading relationships between Bimin-Kuskusmin and Oksapmin groups (Poole 1981). Prior to the location of a mission and the government patrol post in Oksapmin territory, Bimin-Kuskusmin were generally the dominant partners in exchange with Oksapmin. First to acquire new trade goods and money, the Oksapmin, however, have disengaged themselves from certain aspects of traditional trade, thus affecting Bimin-Kuskusmin relationships with other ethnic groups to the south and west, and they have diminished the formerly critical role of Bimin-Kuskusmin in regional trade. In addition, Oksapmin groups with whom the Bimin-Kuskusmin intermarry have begun to demand quantities of European goods and money somewhat beyond the means of Bimin-

SYMBOLIC PRODUCTION AND CONSUMPTION   99

Kuskusmin to readily supply. The recent ascendancy of Oksapmin in political, economic, and ritual power is thus central to Bimin-Kuskusmin perception that Oksapmin witches are attacking them with increasing malevolence (Poole 1981). It is in this context that Bimin-Kuskusmin ritually transform the identity of Oksapmin victims through cannibalistic acts that obliterate destructive male and female substances and enhance the reproductive powers of Bimin-Kuskusmin and their pandanus trees.

The situation is made particularly urgent by the predicament that Bimin-Kuskusmin obtain wives from the Oksapmin, their more numerous neighbors, the bearers of a sweet potato culture (Bimin-Kuskusmin rely more on taro), who rarely become bilingual in Bimin-Kuskusmin, although 75% of the latter are said to be bilingual in Oksapmin.[3] Obsessive ritual attention to the particularities of sexuality and fertility now find their place in the increasing concern of Bimin-Kuskusmin to transform and efface aspects of a people who threaten their very identity, but on whom they reluctantly depend.

A consideration of the historical processes that contribute to Gimi concepts of cannibalim returns the present discussion to the earlier question of whether rituals reflect social relationships, or act so as to mask or deny them. Gillison's challenging analysis presents us with three kinds of evidence: a myth said to tell of the origin of women's cannibalism (with its remarkable parallels to men's mythic theft from women of sacred bamboo flutes), informants' accounts of cannibal rituals no longer practiced, and current death rites which include women's playlets of their chaotic alimentary attack on dummy male corpses. The myth is said to serve as a stylized description or "explanation" of informants' accounts of events that formerly occurred, while the present-day death ritual is treated as an occasion for detecting fragments of the ritualized ingestion of bodies pictured in both myths and informants' accounts of defunct mortuary rituals.

There is, in effect, a fourth source of evidence of cannibal behavior running through Gillison's paper, and that concerns both the ethnographic and epidemiological evidence of who ate whom.

---

[3] Tom Moylan, personal communication. For an earlier discussion of this point, see Lindenbaum (forthcoming).

These additional lines of information describe a pattern of cannibal consumption somewhat at variance with the one presented in myth, current ritual, or accounts of rituals said to have occurred in the past. In contrast to the image of female cannibals ingesting the bodies of in-groups males, we find here that adult men and young children of both sexes are cannibal participants and that adult female cannibals ate the bodies of women as well as those of men. This paradox offers us an opportunity of reconsidering the problem of whether myth and ritual are ways of knowing the world or of hiding it.

The heavy symbolic load in favor of the cultural view that Gimi women were the eaters of Gimi men is a significant focus of Gillison's essay, and the most illuminating moments of the analysis follow from her pursuit of the connecting threads of symbolic reasoning to be found in myth and ritual. The story of the women's "stealing back" of male corpses does seem to echo the earlier, male theft of the sacred penis/flute, the myth of the origin of culture — a battle, one might add, played out among a limited cast of kin. Brothers and sisters appear to be the central participants in the two myths, although mothers join the contest in the myth of the women cannibals, as well as in the present-day mortuary rituals where women enact the social disruption that their threat of symbolic reincorporation portends. We detect both a symbolic resonance and a situational echo in the various mythic and ritual episodes, but an answer to the myth/reality problem may require a stronger historical stand as we look more closely at the conjunction of myth telling, ritual performance, and historical action.

A focus on the historical dimension of social processes shows people in local groups accommodating to events that initiate or transform their relationships with outsiders (or insiders) at the same time as they modify their relationships with one another. Fijian rituals of cannibalism, for example, are composed of the interactions among the "social cum cosmic categories" of immigrant chiefs, foreign warriors, and indigenous members of the land, while the Fijian cannibal myth distills the new system of relationships and cultural understandings (without dwelling on the internal conflicts and contradictions) that the intrusion of the immigrants brought about. Sherbro also define cannibal dangers in continuously changing political contexts that include immigrants, rising members of their own community, and colonial courts of appeal, just as Arapesh and Bimin-Kuskusmin beliefs about cannibalism restate cultural and personal identity in the face of a shifting universe of human, semihuman, and nonhuman impingements. In this light, it may be suggested that Gimi cannibal beliefs and rituals might also be seen as a sediment of their progressive involvement with outsiders such as the Chimbu, who in the 1950s were trading for feathers in the heavily forested regions of the Eastern Highlands.[4]

The Gimi material, presented by Gillison in enticing abundance, offers an opportunity for attempting a historical interpretation of the symbolic logic that her analysis reveals. One clue to an important historical transition lies in the formation that some 30 years ago, before the increase in numbers of domesticated pigs, marsupials were the main source of ritual meat. Culturally speaking, pigs do seem to have taken the place of possums in the overall symbolic scheme (pigs = marsupials = human fetus = internalized male), but in "real" life, the two animals differ in significant ways. Possums are acquired in relatively short-term episodes of hunting by moles, while pigs are the product of relatively long-term intensive female labor, involving increased production of food for the pigs as well as new tasks of animal tending. This entails an incremental though major shift in the social relationships of men and women in production, a shift that is glossed over by the cultural "sleight of hand" involved in symbolic logic, as well as in the "echoes" among the elements of ritual events. The increased demand for the labor of one group by another, an inflection of gender roles, is apparently subsumed into and largely engineered through mythic and ritual communication which does not directly address the compelling matters at hand.

In addition to Gillison's persuasive analysis of its symbolic import, the myth of the cannibal women may be seen as relating to this historic circumstance. The myth is not so much concerned, then, with the origin of female cannibalism (which appears to be in place when the story begins), as with the ritual presentation of pigs to women, a kind of ritual coercion. Additional ethnographic or historical data might help to tease out the sequence of events leading up to the in-

---

[4] Paula Brown (personal communication).

troduction of this ritual, so that we might come to understand more about the components of rituals themselves, as well as their relationship to myths and to extraritual events. The epidemiology of kuru (the central nervous system disorder afflicting people in the region) provides one piece of the puzzle, for we know that only one case of kuru has occurred in a Gimi male born since 1952 (Tarr 1980). That is, Gimi males, but not females, appear to have avoided human flesh since that date, which is approximately the time when Gimi turned their attention to domestic pig production. The ritual, along with the "doctrinal" aspects of the myth, thus appears to resolve the dilemma facing Gimi men in the early 1950s, as pigs were becoming the new currency of the region. How could they keep a relative monopoly of pork consumption, retain the notion that men create culture, and at the same time turn women's cognitive and emotional attention (not to speak of their labor) toward the animals themselves? Gillison's analysis captures the psychodynamics of this achievement, part of which involves the casuistic message that pigs should join that great chain of symbolic beings which women "process" in the interests of cultural life and social order. (It is interesting to note that Bimin-Kuskusmin ritual cannibalism also requires a "second meal" of selected wild boar and cassowary parts, thought to culturally reconstitute Bimin-Kuskusmin males and females, underlining Tuzin's observation concerning the psychological complexity associated with eating and emotion).

A focus upon symbols in historical contexts appears to open up the conjunction of myth, ritual, and social experience, and provides a small viewing station from which to examine the relations among the parts. Myth, ritual, and the extraritual experiences of people in historically grounded modes of production differentially shape cultural conceptions and values, such that one is not a direct printout of the other. Myth-telling, ritual, and extraritual activities assemble different interest groups and combinations of interest groups, each with its particular form of communication and intentional message. In the female creation myth, told by Gimi women to Gimi women, a bride enlivens the corpse of her brother by placing his body in a tree hollow, and striking the sealed trunk with a stick. Men's initiation stories, on the other hand, tell of men bringing about the rebirth of the spirits of the dead, as well as the emergence of adult men from less-than-male novices. These diverging accounts, told to different audiences, depend on the parsimonious imagery of trees, treetops, and the explosive flights of birds, used to convey different understandings about the key contributions to Gimi life (female regeneration through incest, male homosexual creation). When men and women constitute both audience and actors in a ritual event, however, the message relates to social "reality" in a different manner again. The riotous playlet witnessed at the mortuary feast, for instance, shows men and women expressing "unspoken coopera-tion in the enactment of conflict." Here, women act out their desire to reincorporate certain men,[5] predominantly male siblings. Still, men hold the upper hand, having freed themselves from this in-cestuous eating by slipping pigs in as their symbolic alternates. The consequences of the power play are protested to a degree by the women's burlesque treatment of their desires, but the ritual enact-ment of the contradictory interests of all of the participants, re-solved publicly in favor of men, itself constitutes an additional contri-bution to Gimi ideology concerning the relations between the sexes. The Bimin-Kuskusmin Great Pandanus rituals similarly give visible expression to the combined male and female orchestration of Bimin-Kuskusmin conceptions of gender and self. While ap-preciating the artifice of symbolic production, or becoming aware, as Sahlins says, that "the *mana* of the social contract lies in sym-bolism itself" (p. 74), it is also evident that the symbolic process in-volves a complex interplay among myth, ritual, and event, with their variable participants and audiences, each refracting different-ly on the other. Myths appear to "etherize" the contradictions that rituals continue to enact, suggesting that although ritual is not con-sidered to be a discursive form of communication, ritual perfor-mance is closer than myth to active political debate.

A view of the symbolic process in historical focus also reveals that the development of the cultural understandings encoded in myths rises out of an emergency, a challenge to the status quo, and pro-ceeds by a kind of borrowing from earlier symbolic assumptions. The traditional Fijian myth of the origin of cannibalism, a product

---

[5] The theme of sisters eating brothers again seems prominent. Among neighboring Fore, women tell of sisters and sons' wives having the right to eat the upper portion of their brothers bodies and brother's wives, the portions below the navel. Moreover, although some men were cannibals, brothers were forbidden to eat any part of their sisters.

of the arrival of the immigrant "tabuas" on indigenous shores, portrays an archetypical situation to which subsequent ceremonies and transactions (such as turtle fishing) refer. Similarly, the flute myth of the Eastern Highlands provides a cultural paradigm (forged in a social context about which we can now only speculate) upon which to construct future messages. The Gimi myth of the cannibal women, a kind of flute myth in reverse, is thus instantly discerned as an unacceptable theft of the sacred flute/penis, properly followed by a "disciplinary" second meal. The statements by male and female informants that "it was wrong to eat a man and pigs at the same time" and "first we ate the man, the pigs came later," can be thus taken in the double sense of an alimentary correction and a sequence of events. The "second meal," along with its mythic justification, is to be seen as an early component in the development of the ceremonial exchange of pigs in this part of the Highlands.[6] The Arapesh refusal to think that the Japanese had become cannibals in order to survive a famine similarly derives its significance, as Tuzin shows, from the resonance of an earlier image of cannibalism in the Arapesh conceptual scheme. Like the Fijian myth of origin, and the Gimi myth of the cannibal women (itself a "derivative" of the myth of the sacred flutes), an Arapesh origin myth poses a cannibal exchange that gives way to the civilizing gift of pork, a primal scene (composed of important organizational and subsistence strategies), upon which subsequent cultural understandings are constructed.

A full symbolic analysis requires that we locate the "emergency" conditions that give rise to contradictory interests among individuals and groups and that we further refine our understanding of the dynamic interactions among myth-telling, ritual performance, and other social behaviors in different historical contexts. Hidden messages about ethnic encounters, gender struggles, and the contest between elders and youths come tied to a rather limited set of symbolic counters. One is struck by the economy of the means by which the elements present in the myths of origin reappear in subsequent myths and rituals, as different interest groups attempt to resolve their current predicaments and influence the situation in their

---

[6] In December 1971, David Boyd was present when the Ilakia Awa (eastern neighbors of the Fore and the Gimi) decided to increase the number of pigs in their subsistence strategy by borrowing and performing the Fore flute ritual complex. See Boyd (1974).

favor. By a kind of symbolic fission and fusion, the same images develop a cumulative significance, a semantic efficacy that gels in moral opinion and conscious belief.

The present collection of papers indicates that myth, ritual, and social practice act in tandem at a particular moment, but make different contributions to what we think of as ideology and institutional change. Some recent works suggest that unconscious or preconscious understandings of later, more formal behaviors are prefigured in certain modes of discourse, such as iconographic representation (Bucher 1981) and literature (Williams 1980). If this is the case, the path ahead requires that we examine the different modes of discourse themselves, in addition to our current "full hand" of a psychologically and historically informed analysis. To say that anthropology is faced with a myth/reality problem appears to be an oversimplification of this more complicated and more interesting unscrambling assignment.

REFERENCES

BLOCH, MAURICE.   1977.   The Past and the Present in the Present. *Man* 12(2): 278–292.

BOURDILLON, M. F. C.   1978.   Knowing the World or Hiding It: A Response to Maurice Bloch. *Man* 13(4):591–599.

BOYD, DAVID J.   1974.   "We Must Follow the Fore": Pig Husbandry Intensification Among the Ilakia Awa. Contribution to Symposium on The Use and Management of Pigs in the New Guinea Highlands, American Anthropological Association Meetings, Mexico City.

BUCHER, BERNADETTE.   1981.   *Icon and Conquest. A Structural Analysis of the Illustrations of de Bry's Great Voyages.* (Basia Miller Gulati, trans.) Chicago: University of Chicago Press.

DORNSTREICH, M. D. and G. E. B. MORREN.   1974.   Does New Guinea Cannibalism Have Nutritional Value? *Human Ecology* 2:1–12.

HARNER, M.   1977.   The Ecological Basis for Aztec Sacrifice. *American Ethnologist* 4:117–135.

HARRIS, M.   1977.   *Cannibals and Kings.* New York: Random House.

LANGNESS, L. L.   1976.   Discussion. *Man and Woman in the New Guinea Highlands,* (P. Brown and G. Buchbinder, eds.), pp. 96–106. Washington, D.C.: American Anthropological Association.

LÉVI-STRAUSS, C., M. GODELIER, M. AUGÉ.   1976.   Anthropology, History and Ideology. *Critique of Anthropology* 2(6):44–55.

LEWIS, I. M.   1977.   Introduction. *Symbols and Sentiments. Cross-cultural Studies in Symbolism* (Ioan Lewis, ed.), pp. 1–24. London: Academic Press.

LINDENBAUM, SHIRLEY.   In press.   Images of the Sorcerer in Papua New Guinea. *Social Analysis.*.

106   SHIRLEY LINDENBAUM

ORTNER, SHERRY B. and WHITEHEAD, HARRIET.   1981.   *Sexual Meanings. The Cultural Construction of Gender and Sexuality.* Cambridge, Eng.: Cambridge University Press.

POOLE, FITZ JOHN PORTER.   1981.   *Tamam:* Ideological and Sociological Configurations of "Witchcraft" among Bimin-Kuskusmin. *Social Analysis.* 8:58–76.

SILVERMAN, SYDEL.   1981.   Rituals of Inequality: Stratification and Symbol in Central Italy. *Social Inequality: Comparative and Development Approaches.* (Gerald D. Berreman, ed.), pp. 163–181. New York: Academic Press.

TARR, PHILLIP I.   1980.   The Geography and Epidemiology of the Disappearance of Kuru. Dissertation submitted for Doctor of Medicine, Yale University School of Medicine.

TUZIN, DONALD F.   1976.   *The Ilahita Arapesh: Dimensions of Unity.* Berkeley: University of California Press.

WILLIAMS, RAYMOND.   1980.   *Problems in Materialism and Culture.* London: Verso.